IRONOPOLIS

THE ARCHITECTURE OF MIDDLESBROUGH

MICHAEL JOHNSON

AMBERLEY

First published 2020

Amberley Publishing, The Hill, Stroud
Gloucestershire GL5 4EP

www.amberley-books.com

British Library Cataloguing in Publication Data.
A catalogue record for this book is available from the British Library.

ISBN 978 1 4456 7042 3 (print)
ISBN 978 1 4456 7043 0 (ebook)

Typesetting by Aura Technology and Software Services, India.
Printed in Great Britain.

Contents

Introduction

Middlesbrough lies on the south bank of the River Tees in the north-east of England. Its dramatic position between the industrial river valley of Teesside and the wild expanse of the Cleveland Hills is matched by an equally extraordinary history. Unlike most urban settlements, Middlesbrough did not evolve over centuries, but had a specific genesis, created by capitalist enterprise. In 1828, a group of Quaker businessmen recognised the potential of this flat, marshy area close to the mouth of the Tees and determined to establish a new port for the shipment of coal. Conceived and built by its industrial pioneers, Middlesbrough was a Victorian new town, planned on a strict grid system. One of Britain's fastest growing settlements, Middlesbrough became a world-leading centre of iron and steel production, earning itself the epithet 'Ironopolis'.

Expressing this rapid expansion, Middlesbrough's historic architecture is surprisingly rich. From the superb Victorian Town Hall to the iconic Transporter Bridge, Middlesbrough's buildings exude civic pride and industrial prowess. The town boasts an incredible variety of churches and chapels, many of them displaying stylistic influences found nowhere else in the North East. Central Middlesbrough is fortunate to possess two churches by Temple Moore (1856–1920), perhaps the last great architect of the Gothic Revival. Another treasure is the former office of Bell Brothers, the only surviving commercial building by the Arts and Crafts pioneer Philip Webb (1831–1915). After a period of decline and the loss of much of its Victorian architecture, the turn of the millennium has seen Middlesbrough enhance its reputation with ambitious new projects such as the Middlesbrough Institute of Modern Art and public sculptures by internationally renowned artists.

This book examines Middlesbrough's architectural history through a selective survey of its finest buildings. The entries are arranged chronologically to trace the town's development from *c.* 1830 to the present. Middlesbrough has suffered more than most towns from destructive planning decisions and an apparent disregard, within some circles, for its built heritage. For this reason, any appraisal of Middlesbrough's architecture must address notable buildings that have been lost, as well as those that survive within the changing townscape.

The name Middlesbrough is derived from 'Mydilsburgh', as the area was known in Anglo-Saxon times, referring to its middle location between the religious centres of Durham and Whitby. In AD 686, St Cuthbert consecrated a monastic cell on this site at the request of the Abbess of Whitby. The cell became a priory church dedicated to St Hilda in 1119, maintained by twelve Benedictine monks from Whitby. It remained there until it was dissolved by Thomas Cromwell in the time of Henry VIII.

In 1801, Middlesbrough was a farm with a population of twenty-five people. By the end of the century, it had been transformed into an industrial metropolis of 90,000 inhabitants. This meteoric growth was unprecedented in British urban history. The world's first railway was built between Stockton and Darlington in 1825 to transport coal from the Weardale district of Durham to the River Tees. As trade developed, it became clear that a new port was required south of the river. On 2 August 1828, Joseph Pease (1799–1872), a Quaker banker, colliery owner and shareholder in the Stockton and Darlington Railway, sailed up the river to find a suitable site for new coal staithes. He wrote in his diary that night:

> I took a boat, and entering the Teesmouth sailed up to Middlesbrough to take view of the proposed termination of the completed ending of the railway, and was pleased with the place altogether. Its adaptation far exceeded my anticipations. I was fancying the coming of a day when the bare fields we then were traversing would be covered with a busy multitude, and numerous vessels crowding to these banks denoting a busy seaport.

Led by Pease, a group of six businessmen established a company called the Owners of the Middlesbrough Estate in 1829 and bought the farmstead for £30,000. Shipping staithes were constructed from plans by Timothy Hackworth (1786–1850) and the Stockton and Darlington Railway was extended to Middlesbrough in 1830, ensuring that Pease's prophecy would be fulfilled.

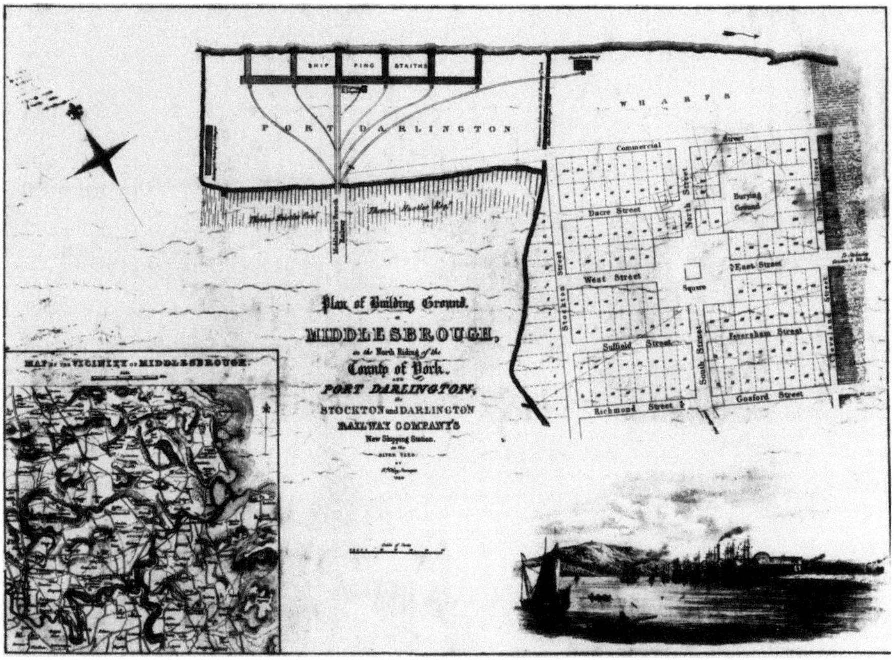

Map of Middlesbrough in 1850, showing the grid plan of the early streets. (Middlesbrough Libraries and Information)

The Owners set about developing a town to supply labour for the new port. The plan was devised by the company's land surveyor Richard Otley, based on that of a Roman fort. Streets were laid out in a grid-iron pattern around a market square and businesses rapidly bought up plots in order to capitalise on the influx of workers. The first residents came mainly from Yorkshire and the North East, but migrants from Scotland, Wales, Ireland and European countries soon followed. In its rapid growth and layout, Middlesbrough was akin to the gold rush towns of the American West. The extraordinary pace of this development is expressed in the Latin motto the town adopted in 1830, *Erimus* ('We shall be').

The first Town Hall was erected in 1846 as the centrepiece of the planned town. An impression of Middlesbrough's urban character in this era can be gained from the Georgian-style houses surviving in Queen's Terrace. The earliest public buildings reflect the classical style that was prevalent in this era. Developing later than other towns, however, Middlesbrough never became a major centre of classicism as did Newcastle to the north. Instead, its architecture reflects the more eclectic tastes of the mid and late Victorian periods. Twelve Improvement Commissioners were appointed by an Act of Parliament in 1841 to improve the town by setting standards in planning, building, road-making and drainage. However, Middlesbrough's explosive growth and the development of heavy industry inevitably brought the evils of overcrowding, poor sanitation and omnipresent pollution.

Middlesbrough's Iron Age began in 1841, when Heinrich Wilhelm Ferdinand Bölckow (1806–78) and John Vaughan (1799–1868) established an iron foundry

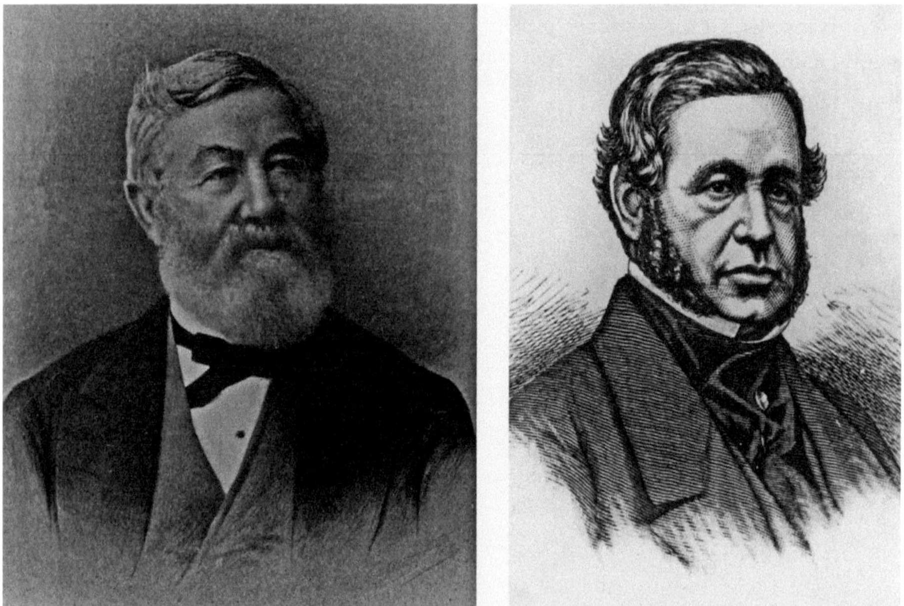

Pioneering ironmasters Henry Bolckow (left) and John Vaughan (right). (Middlesbrough Libraries and Information)

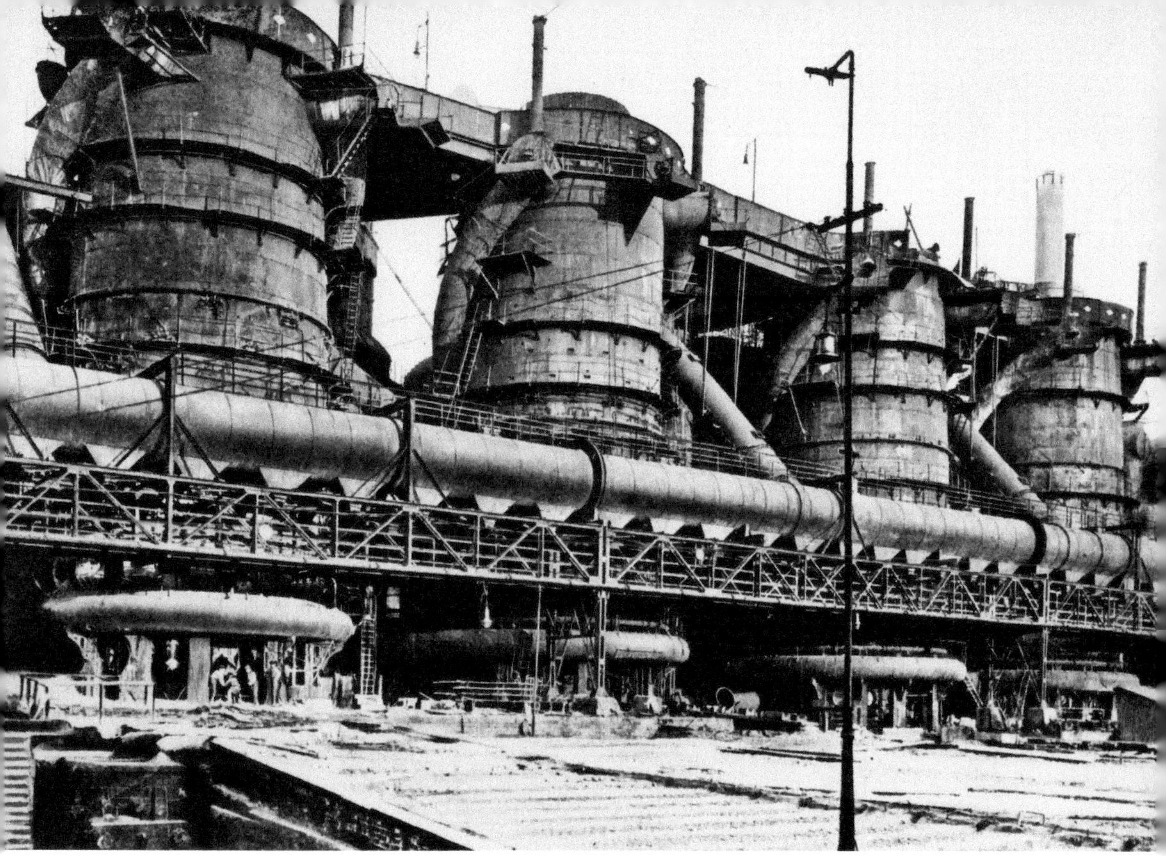

Towering blast furnaces at the Acklam Iron Works. (Middlesbrough Libraries and Information)

and rolling mill in Vulcan Street. Henry Bolckow, as he Anglicised his name, was a successful German accountant who had money to invest in new enterprises. Vaughan had much experience in the production of iron, as well as scientific knowledge as a metallurgist. These were the ironmasters whose vision and enterprise transformed Middlesbrough into the greatest iron-making district in the world.

In 1850, Vaughan discovered major reserves of ironstone, a sedimentary rock containing a compound from which iron can be smelted, in the Eston Hills south of Middlesbrough. The discovery prompted Bolckow and Vaughan to build Teesside's first blast furnace in 1851. Iron was in great demand for the nation's industries and the expansion of railways. Numerous blast furnaces opened around Middlesbrough, as well as over 100 puddling furnaces for processing the iron. By 1865, Middlesbrough had become the world's largest producer of iron, generating a third of Britain's output. In 1881, newspaper baron Sir Hugh Gilzean Reid (1836–1911), echoing the journalist George Holyoake (1817–1906), exclaimed:

> The iron of Eston has diffused itself all over the world. It furnishes the railways of the world; it runs by Neapolitan and papal dungeons; it startles the bandit in his haunt in Cicilia; it crosses over the plains of Africa; it stretches over the plains of India. It has crept out of the Cleveland Hills where it has slept since Roman days, and now like a strong and invincible serpent, coils itself around the world.

As industry thrived, the Victorian capitalists who commanded its Vulcanic infrastructure became a hegemonic ruling class. Bolckow was elected as the town's first mayor in 1853 and its first MP in 1868, Middlesbrough having become a parliamentary borough the previous year. Vital public amenities were provided through the philanthropy of Middlesbrough's industrial elite, including hospitals, schools, libraries and places of worship. In 1862, surveying the town's transformation into a world-class industrial powerhouse, the great Victorian statesman William E. Gladstone, then Chancellor of the Exchequer, exclaimed, 'This remarkable place, the youngest child of England's enterprise, is an infant, but if an infant, an infant Hercules.'

As Middlesbrough grew, the centre of commerce shifted to the area south of the railway line. Albert, Marton and Linthorpe Roads were developed from 1856, with a dense infill of buildings in a range of fashionable architectural styles, providing premises for new businesses. Linthorpe Road became the primary retail axis. The majestic Royal Exchange opened in 1868, hosting an iron market every Tuesday and Friday. This area became the focus for the iron and steel trade, particularly after the neo-Gothic railway station was built nearby in 1873–77. Banking and financial institutions clustered around the Exchange and the architectural character of this vicinity still proclaims the wealth and power that Middlesbrough amassed in this era. A magnificent new Town Hall and municipal buildings were erected in Corporation Road in 1883–89, confirming that the heart of Middlesbrough had shifted away from the embryonic town founded by Pease and his associates to this new urban centre.

By the 1870s, the demand for iron was declining in favour of steel, a stronger and more resilient metal. For example, the North Eastern Railway began using steel for its rails in 1870. Recognising the need to adapt, Bolckow and Vaughan opened the first steel plant in Middlesbrough to use the Bessemer process, an inexpensive means of producing steel by oxidising molten pig iron. Steel gradually replaced iron as the lifeblood of the town. The successful transition to steel-making ensured that Middlesbrough continued to play a key role in heavy manufacturing into the twentieth century.

The most visible monuments to Middlesbrough's supremacy in steel production are the gargantuan bridges spanning the Tees. The Transporter Bridge (1911) was designed to facilitate crossings without impeding traffic on the river and remains the salient icon of Middlesbrough. Equally innovative was the Tees (Newport) Bridge (1934), England's first vertical lifting bridge. On the far side of the world, the Sydney Harbour Bridge (1932) was built by Dorman Long & Co. using 51,000 tons of Teesside steel.

As in the Victorian era, Middlesbrough's industrial titans were active as philanthropists. The Dorman Museum (1904) was provided by Sir Arthur John Dorman, co-founder of Dorman Long. Further downstream, the company built the industrial village of Dormanstown to house its workers. Planned by renowned architects Stanley D. Adshead (1868–1946) and Stanley C. Ramsey (1882–1968) with Sir Patrick Abercrombie (1879–1957), the village represents a fascinating interplay of tradition and modernity. The prevailing aesthetic was a simplified neo-Georgian style, but many of the dwellings were innovative 'Dorlonco houses', built using prefabricated steel components.

Middlesbrough was the first major British town to be bombed during the Second World War, its steel-making capacity, docks and railways making it a prime target. Seventy-six people were killed, and 318 buildings were destroyed during these attacks. Seeking to build a better future, Middlesbrough was the first town in the country to make a complete urban survey. Devised by a team led by Max Lock (1909–88) in 1944, the Middlesbrough Survey incorporated sociological research and formed the basis for post-war development. Much early and mid-Victorian housing was demolished and the town centre was redeveloped with new housing and commercial buildings. Modern shopping areas were planned as pedestrian precincts and tower blocks such as the former Corporation House (1974) rose above the Victorian townscape. However, many of these developments had an adverse effect on Middlesbrough's architectural heritage, giving parts of its central area an atmosphere of dystopian bleakness.

The most devastating intrusion was the construction of the A66 flyover in the 1980s. Built as part of the 'Northern Route' bypass, the elevated concrete and brick roadway cut through the historic core of Middlesbrough, destroying many fine buildings, including the Royal Exchange. The bypass has reinforced the separation of the Victorian ironmasters' district from the modern town centre and aggressively overshadows the historic buildings that narrowly escaped its onslaught.

The last decades of the twentieth century witnessed the gradual collapse of the industries that made Middlesbrough famous throughout the world. Decades of decline culminated in the closure of the Teesside steelworks in 2015, with the loss of over 2,000 jobs. In response to these changes, various regeneration projects have been launched in order to stimulate social and economic growth. Public art has been at the centre of many such projects. Middlesbrough boasts England's only public sculpture by pop artists Claes Oldenburg and Coosje Van Bruggen, the *Bottle of Notes* (1993), which alludes to Middlesbrough's famous son, Captain James Cook (1728–79). The *Temenos* sculpture (2010) at Middlehaven was created by artist Anish Kapoor and engineer Cecil Balmond. A constructivist vortex of steel cables, it recalls the area's history of manufacturing and echoes the Transporter Bridge in its taut, vaulting form. Signaling Middlesbrough's ambitions as a twenty-first-century city, the Middlesbrough Institute of Modern Art opened in 2007, within a newly formed public square.

Despite all these changes, Middlesbrough's urban character is still derived from the layout of the planned Victorian town. Much of the historic townscape remains intact, though with a sense of faded grandeur. The buildings erected during the period of economic prosperity constitute an architectural legacy of tremendous innovation and artistry, while the grid-iron streets regularly open up vistas of the distant Cleveland Hills, the dramatic landscape that cradles this remarkably industrious town.

Acklam Hall (1680–83)

Middlesbrough's oldest domestic building is Acklam Hall, which pre-dates the modern town. A house and estate known as Acklam Hall is recorded in the Domesday Book of 1086. The name 'Acklam' is derived from the Anglo-Saxon for 'place of oaks'. The estate passed to the Boynton family at the time of Henry I. In 1612, Sir Francis Boynton rented the estate to William Hustler, a wealthy draper from Bridlington. Hustler bought the entire estate in 1637 to provide a trading base close to the River Tees. The present house was built by Hustler's grandson, William, in 1680–83.

The Restoration mansion has undergone many changes through the centuries. Thomas Hustler, originally of Philadelphia in the USA, carried out extensive alterations in 1845. A contemporary engraving shows a two-storey mansion with a seven-bay frontage, projecting central bay and Dutch gables along the roofline. Further work was carried out in 1910–12 by Sir Walter Henry Brierley (1862–1926) of York, perhaps the leading exponent of the Renaissance style in the North East. Brierley refaced the property in brick with sandstone dressings and added an attic-storey, including Jacobethan-style dormer windows. Coined by John Betjeman, the term 'Jacobethan' refers to an informal style that revived elements of Elizabethan and Jacobean architecture. Brierley introduced the present porch, a splendid frontispiece composed of Ionic columns, ornamental vases and the Hustler coat of arms. He also built a single-storey dining room at the south-east corner, together with new kitchens.

Acklam Hall (1680–83) in its charming grounds.

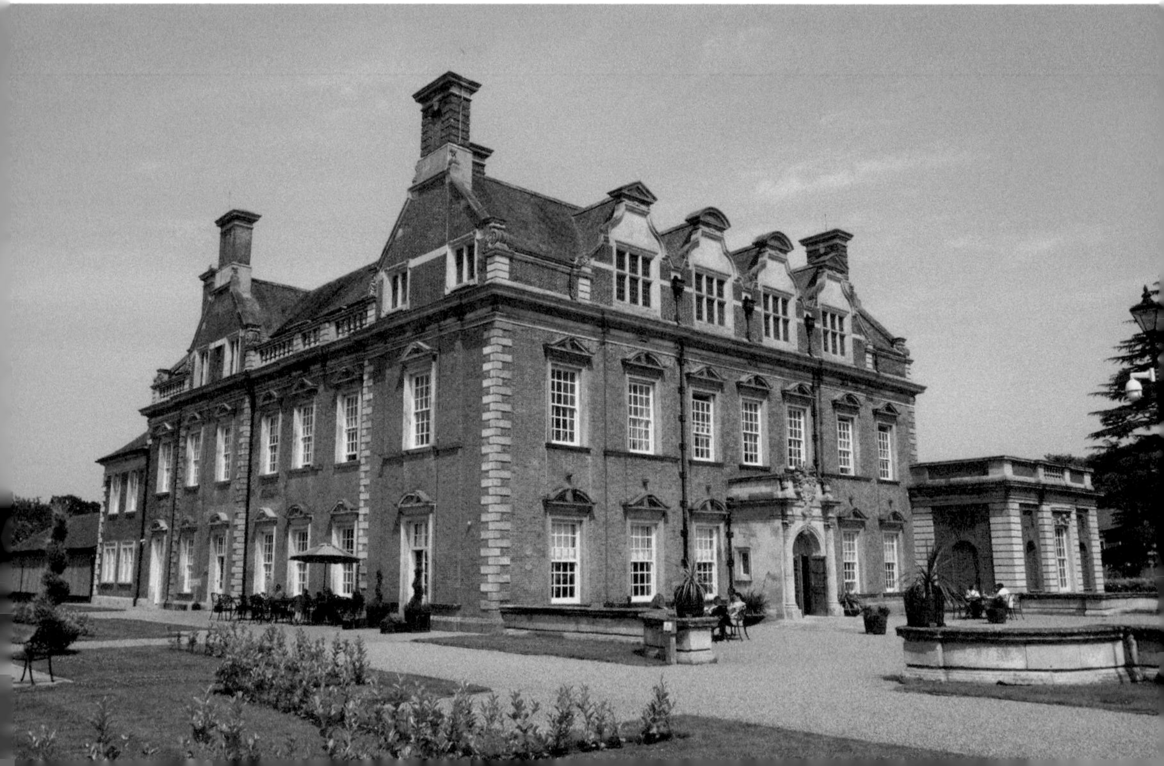

These additions were in the manner of Inigo Jones (1573–1652), who is credited with introducing classical architecture to Britain.

The interior retains decorative features from various periods. The hall is lined with early eighteenth-century wood panelling, but a new ceiling was introduced in 1912, decorated with naturalistic foliage by George Bankart of London. The ceiling in the smoking room dates from *c.* 1740 and features an ornamental frieze, cornice and central medallion. The small boudoir was intended to appeal to 'feminine' taste, with imagery of cherubs, flowers and seashells, all dating from *c.* 1730. Emulating the eighteenth-century interiors, Brierley's dining room features Corinthian pilasters, garlands of flowers and an elliptical panel in the ceiling.

The grand staircase is a superb display of woodcarving. The large square newel posts are topped with ball-and-artichoke finials and the balusters are composed of intertwining double spirals. The climax of this glorious space is the ceiling of 1683, replete with elaborate plasterwork rising to a domed skylight. The most elaborate interior is the drawing room, where the magnificent ceiling features recessed panels around two central octagons. A splendid representation of the Hustler arms proclaims the family's dominion, but, tactfully, does not outshine the richly gilded royal arms of 1684. Amid brilliantly modelled flowers and foliage are suspended doves and griffins.

In 1929, representatives of the Hustler family conveyed Acklam Hall and its estate to Middlesbrough Corporation for £11,500. The house was converted into

The former drawing room of Acklam Hall.

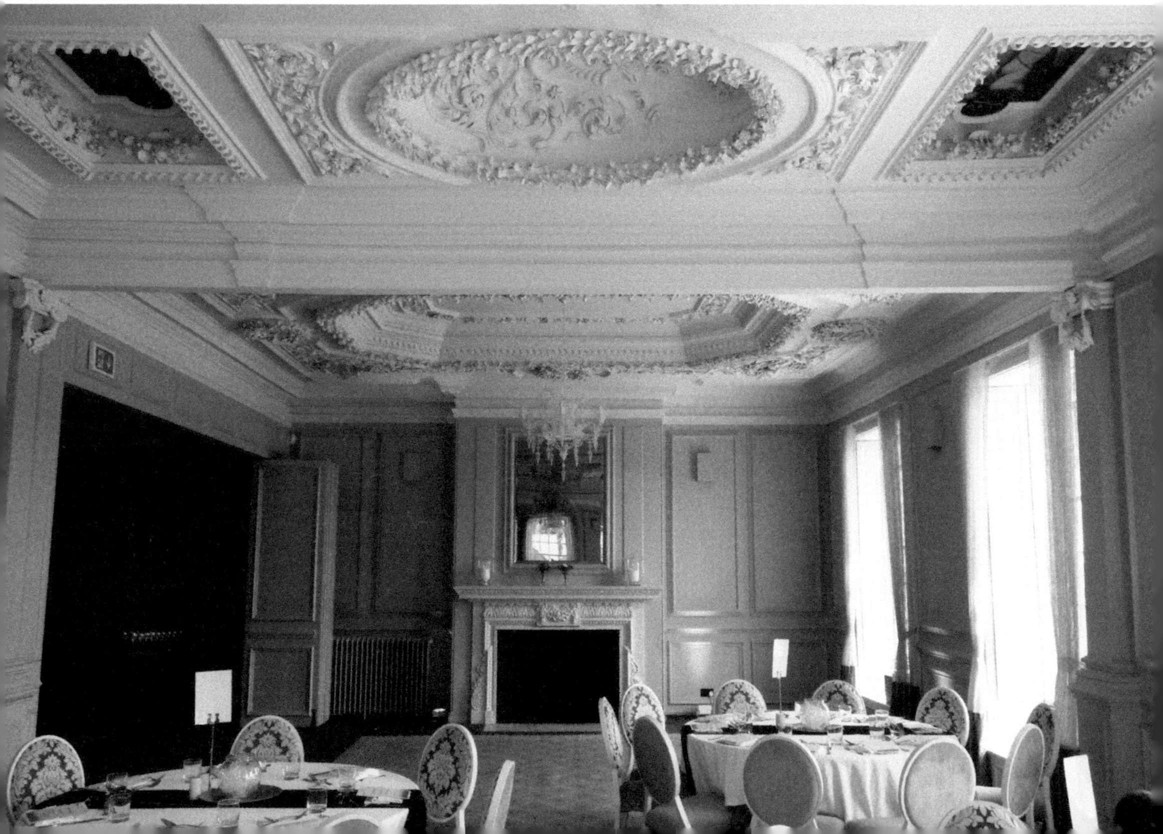

a boys' school in 1935. A single-storey quadrangle containing science laboratories and a gymnasium was built by R. G. Tarran of Hull to designs by the Education Committee's architect P. B. Haswell. Following refurbishment in 2016, Acklam Hall is now an events venue and conference centre. This has safeguarded the building for the foreseeable future, although some of the new design elements seem incongruous. In recognition of its historical and architectural importance, Acklam Hall is the only Grade I listed building in Middlesbrough.

Cleveland Buildings, Cleveland Street (*c.* 1835)

The Cleveland Buildings were originally built as two separate houses in the vicinity of Queen's Square, a genteel residential district. Their significance is due to the fact that they were home to Middlesbrough's pioneering ironmasters Henry Bolckow (in 1841–54) and John Vaughan (in 1841–58). Like the Georgian town houses of a slightly earlier period, they are built of brick and enhanced with stone dressings in the classical style, including doorcases with fluted Tuscan columns and quoins at the corners for reinforcement.

The interior retains some of its original ornamentation, including rich cornices, wood panelling and elliptical-headed alcoves. Remarkably, there is a marble fireplace that was recovered from the *Aquitania* (1913), the third in Cunard's 'grand trio' of ocean liners, after *Mauretania* and *Lusitania*. In 1919, *Aquitania* docked at the Armstrong Whitworth yards in Newcastle to be refitted for post-war

Cleveland Buildings (*c.* 1835), once the residence of Bolckow and Vaughan.

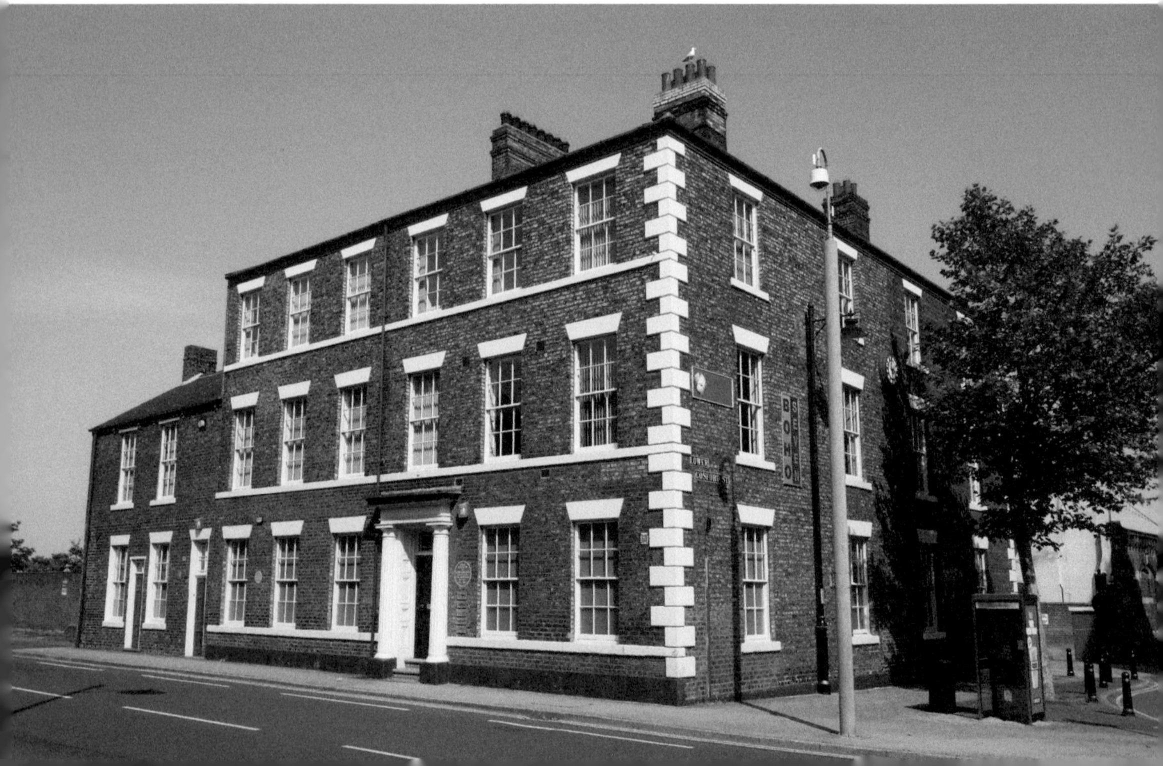

service and it was probably then that the fireplace was removed. The fireplace was designed in the 'Adam style' associated with the Scottish neoclassical architect Robert Adam (1728–92).

Coal Exchange and Hotel, North Street (1835–37)

Enterprising merchants formed the Middlesbrough Exchange Association in 1835 and built an Exchange on North Street where business could be transacted. A monument to Middlesbrough's early development, this imposing classical building was designed by George Burlison of Darlington in 1836. His design is a rare example of Greek Revival architecture in Middlesbrough, a phase of neoclassicism that drew inspiration from the stark, pure forms of Ancient Greek architecture, rather than later Roman models. The style figured prominently in Richard Grainger's celebrated replanning of Newcastle in the 1830s, but it never became dominant in Middlesbrough due to the comparative lateness of the town's foundation.

The principal elevations are faced with sandstone, but the other faces were built of plain brick to reduce costs. The façades are powerfully austere, articulated by giant Doric pilasters and a stark entablature. The ground floor is 'rusticated', a term referring to various masonry techniques designed to convey an effect of strength and power. The doorway, on North Street, takes the form of a portico *in antis*,

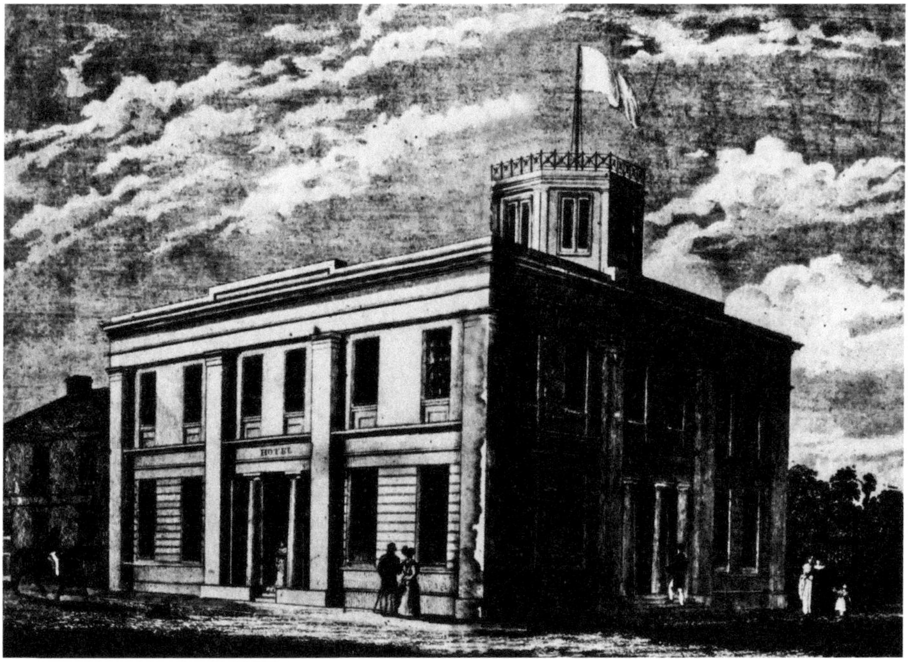

Coal Exchange and Hotel (1835–37), showing the proposed tower. (Middlesbrough Libraries and Information)

meaning that the columns are indented into the façade. This, and the overall severity of the design, indicate the probable influence of Belsay Hall in Northumberland (1810–17), the first Greek Revival building in the North East. Burlison's original design featured an additional entrance on Commercial Street, identical to that on North Street, and a short octagonal tower based loosely on the Tower of the Winds in Athens. However, it seems that these features were omitted during construction.

As a thriving port, Middlesbrough required offices where cargoes could be examined and taxes collected. In 1881, the government purchased the Exchange on North Street for £4,000 to house Customs and Excise officials. The building was used as a Customs House until 1960. The most dignified building of early Middlesbrough, the former Coal Exchange has been transformed into 'Myplace', a £4.3m state-of-the-art youth centre.

Centenary Chapel, Market Place (1833–38)

The Wesleyan Methodists were the first religious community to build a permanent chapel in the new town. The Centenary Chapel was erected in the Market Place, its name commemorating the centenary of John Wesley's evangelical conversion and the beginning of his ministry. Built at a cost of £800, the chapel accommodated 500 people. One of these was the ironmaster John Vaughan, who, having reached his pew, would reputedly adjust his glasses and look around to see which of his foremen were present.

Designed in a bold Renaissance style, the chapel declared its allegiance to Nonconformism, in contrast to the Gothic churches favoured by Anglicans and Catholics. The façade was unconventional, but undeniably powerful in its proportions. The outer bays were framed by tall pilasters (flat-faced columns) and triangular pediments. Unusually, the pilasters featured diamond rustication,

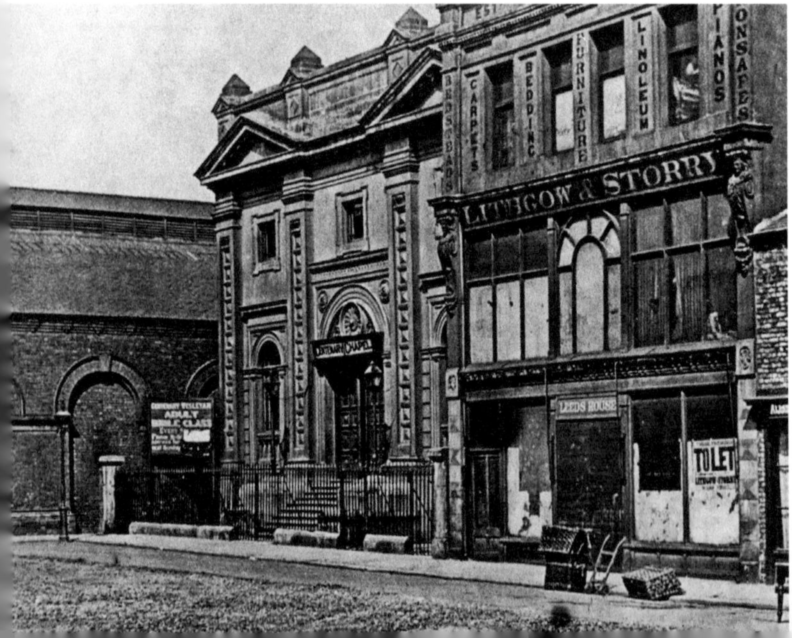

Wesleyan Centenary Chapel (1833–38). (Middlesbrough Libraries and Information)

a form of ornamentation consisting of projecting pyramidal forms, used most prominently at the Palazzo dei Diamanti in Ferrara, Italy (1493–1503). An enlargement and gallery were added in 1848–50 to seat a further 200. The chapel remained in use until 1949, when it was demolished.

St Hilda's Church, Market Place (1838–40)

The founding fathers of Middlesbrough were devout Quakers as well as shrewd businessmen and the Free Churches quickly became a dominant force in the town. There was no Anglican church in the area until St Hilda's was built in 1838–40. Funds of £2,500 were obtained by public subscription and the site was given by Joseph Pease and the Middlesbrough Owners, who stipulated that two pews should be reserved for their use and that the spire should not be less than 120 feet tall.

The original parish church of Middlesbrough, St Hilda's was built in the Market Place at the heart of the new town. The location was significant in that the site

St Hilda's Church (1838–40). (Middlesbrough Libraries and Information)

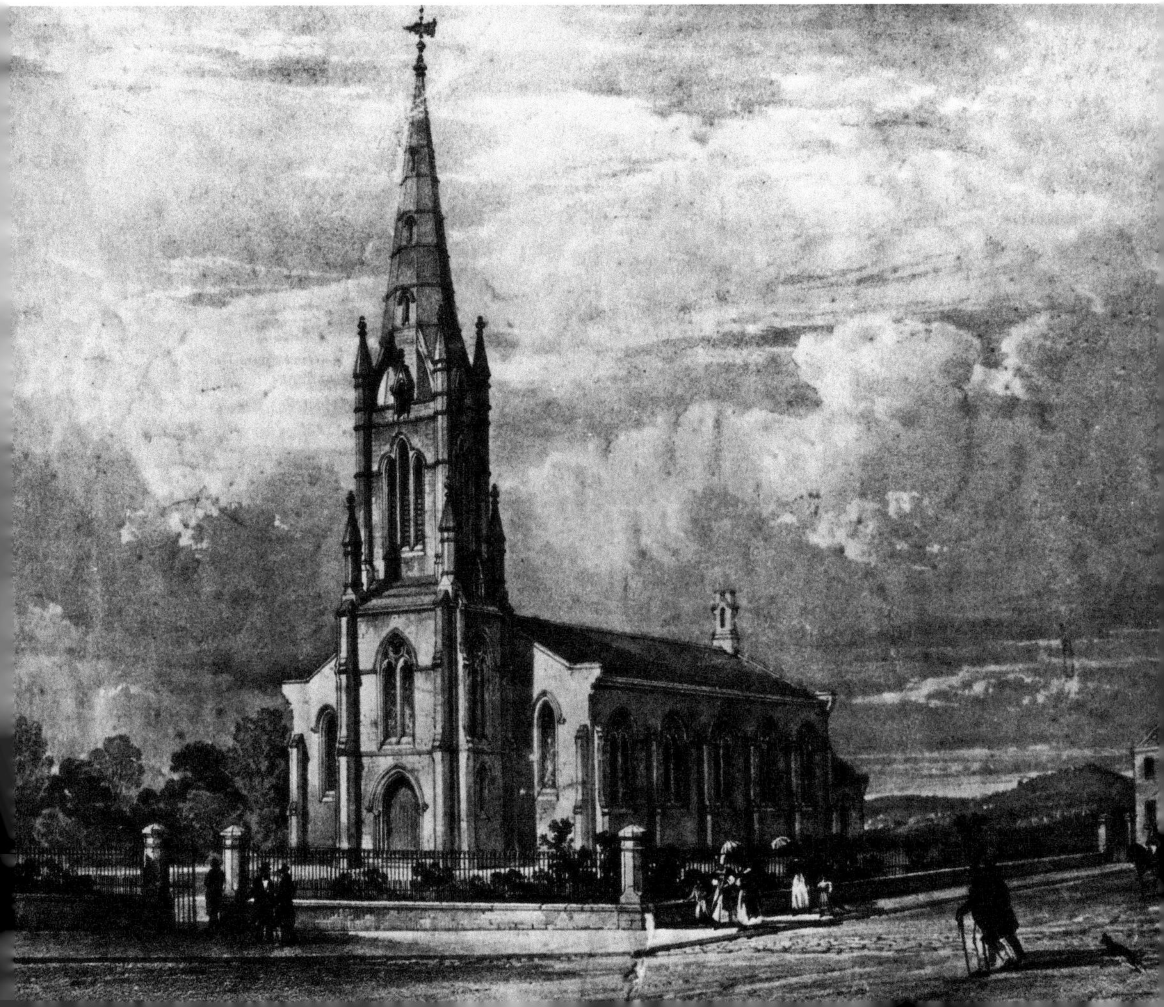

had once been occupied by the medieval village church that preceded the modern town. Designed by father and son architects John (1787–1852) and Benjamin Green (1813–58), it was their only major work in Middlesbrough. The practice was responsible for much of the splendid classical architecture of Newcastle, including the Theatre Royal (1837) and Grey's Monument (1838). Their other main ecclesiastical design was Holy Trinity Church, Stockton (1837).

An early example of Gothic Revival architecture in Middlesbrough, the design resembled Georgian models such as John Dobson's church of St Thomas, Newcastle (1827–30) in its simple rectangular plan, symmetrical massing and western tower. More authentic was the use of Geometrical-style tracery in the windows. The tall spire was braced by flying buttresses, a detail the Greens had used at Stockton.

Many of the interior fittings were donated by the town's ironmasters. The east window was presented by John Vaughan in 1867, while the pulpit (1892) was given in memory of Edward Williams. Most notably, the font of the twelfth-century Benedictine priory was discovered on farmland at Newport and taken to Joseph Pease's house at Darlington, before finally being presented to St Hilda's Church. Round in form and with incised ornamentation, this Norman font is now preserved in the Dorman Museum. The original sanctuary was rebuilt by Middlesbrough architect W. H. Blessley in 1889 at a cost of £695.

St Hilda's Church was eventually closed as Middlesbrough's population migrated south. Deemed unsafe, it was demolished in 1969, destroying a rare ecclesiastical design by an important architectural practice.

Old Town Hall, Market Place (1846)

Still standing as an icon of a former age, Middlesbrough's original Town Hall was erected in the Market Place at the centre of the planned grid pattern of streets. The town's Improvement Commissioners borrowed £2,500 for this structure, comprising a large meeting hall with gallery, a small anteroom and accommodation for the Superintendent of Police. The design was provided by William Lambie Moffatt (1808–82), a Scottish architect based in Doncaster, who was best known for his Greek Revival design for Wakefield Corn Exchange (1836).

Built of stone and white brick, the Town Hall consists of a rectangular main block, with a low extension at the rear, surmounted by a short tower. The simple frontage is in a plain Italian Renaissance style, but follows the basic grammar of Moffatt's design for Wakefield in that the outer bays are treated as pavilions. The tower behind the building was intended as a landmark for Middlesbrough, visible above the surrounding terraces.

In 1853, Middlesbrough received a Charter of Incorporation as a borough and the Town Hall became too small to house the council. The Exchange Hotel in North Street was used as a council chamber, justices' rooms and office for the

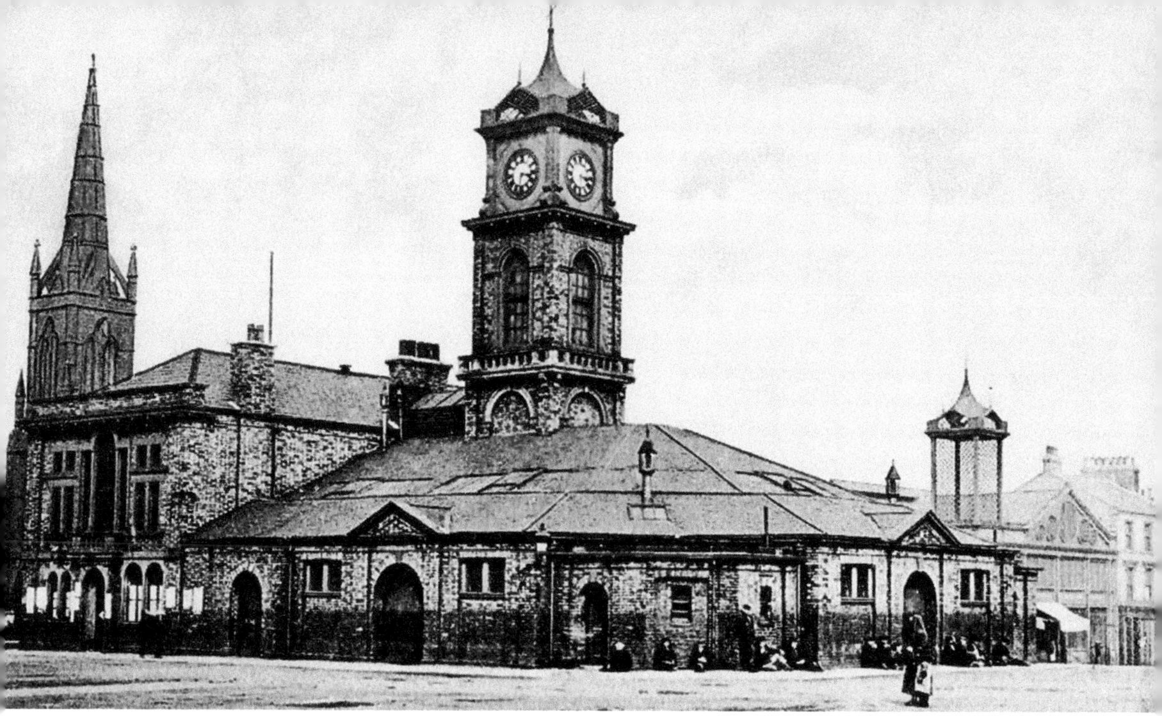

Old Town Hall and Market Place (1846).

Superintendent of Police. As the town began to spread south, a new Town Hall was built in the 1880s. Fortunately, the old Town Hall was retained and bears witness to the town's genesis, but the surrounding streets have long since vanished.

Captain Cook Memorial School, The Grove, Marton (1849–50)

Named after the explorer Captain James Cook, this small parochial school and adjoining schoolhouse form a charming group of buildings in the village of Marton, where Cook was born. The two-storey schoolhouse was designed by Richard Cromwell Carpenter (1812–55) of London and constructed from stone salvaged from Marton Lodge (1790), a local mansion that was destroyed by

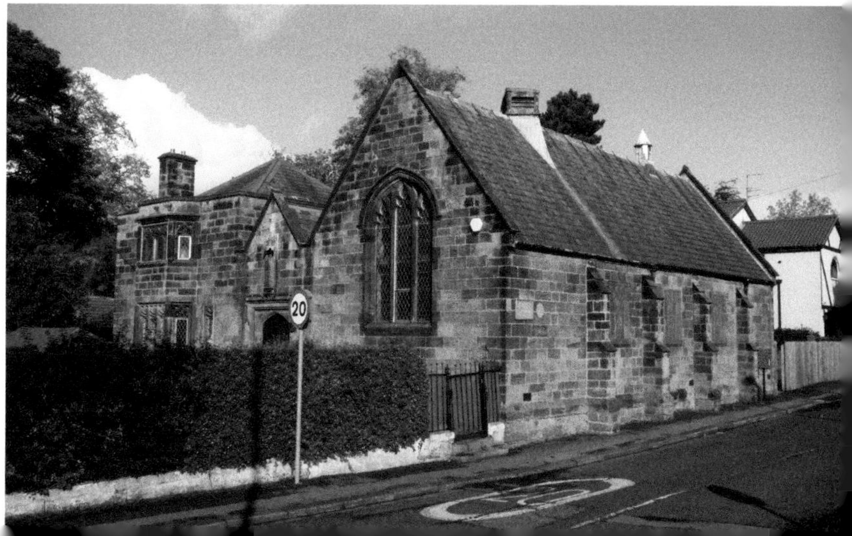

Captain Cook Memorial School (1849–50), now a nursery.

fire in 1832. The school's Tudor Gothic design emulates the charitable almshouses of the late Middle Ages, as advocated by Augustus Pugin (1812–52). A gabled porch and infants' room were added in 1884. The building became a private house in 1961 and is now a nursery school.

Marton Hall (1853)

Marton Hall was built by Middlesbrough's first mayor and MP Henry Bolckow for his own occupation. Bolckow had previously resided in a town house on Cleveland Street, but having amassed a fortune as one of the town's foremost ironmasters, he was able to build a splendid mansion, set within extensive landscaped grounds. This was a common strategy of the Victorian industrial elite, who built grand estates to consolidate their status as Britain's new ruling class. Marton Hall thrived as it received visitors from industry, politics and royalty.

The substantial manor house was built on an estate previously owned by Bartholomew Rudd, a gentleman farmer from Marske. In developing his land, Rudd had demolished the mud and wattle cottage in which the famous explorer Captain James Cook was born. Rudd's own house, Marton Lodge, was destroyed by fire in 1832.

Impressive in its scale and decorative splendour, Marton Hall was, however, rather shapeless in composition. The original building was a relatively subdued Italianate design with pedimented windows and a balustraded parapet around the roofline. The only extravagant feature was an octagonal tower and dome on the north elevation. Extensive remodelling was carried out to prepare the house for a visit from Queen Victoria's son, Prince Arthur, in 1868. The west wing was embellished in French baroque style, with a columned façade, decorous dormer

Marton Hall (1853). (Middlesbrough Libraries and Information)

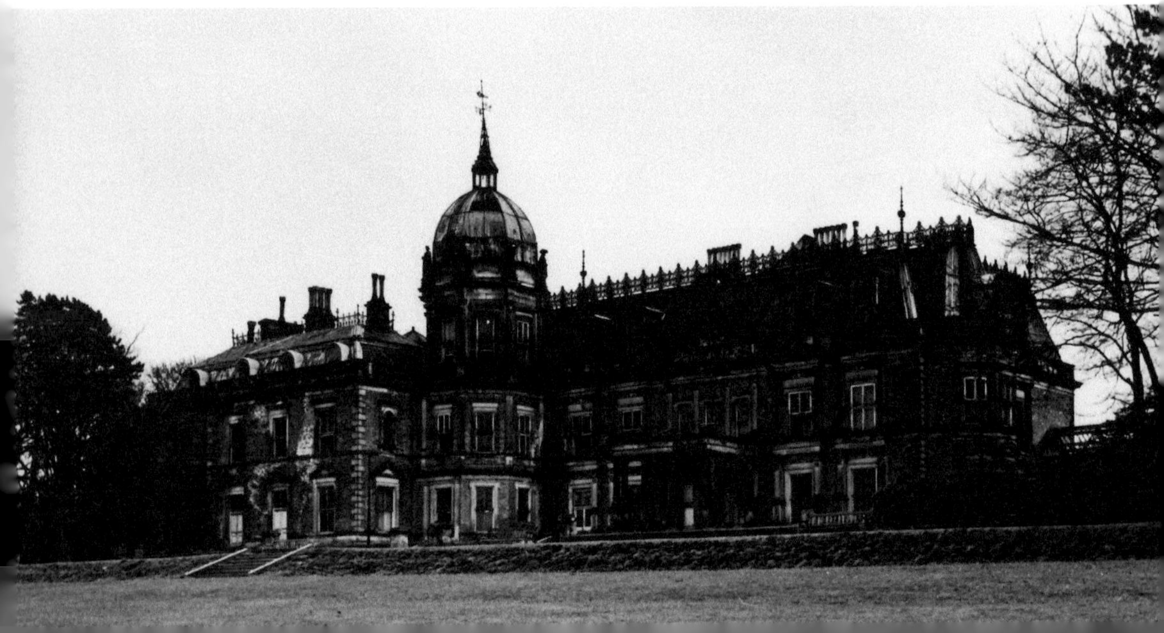

windows and a Mansard roof, a feature named after the French architect François Mansart (1598–1666). The dome was augmented with heroic statues.

The interior was equally magnificent, boasting columns, staircases and balconies of Carrera marble and a tessellated floor of black and white stone. Bolckow reportedly had a fine taste in art, buying several paintings by Turner and Millais, as well as French, Dutch and Flemish curiosities. The collection functioned as a sign of Bolckow's cultivation and social status, since owning artworks was considered an essential part of the cultural makeup of successful men.

After Bolckow's death, the property fell into disrepair. The surrounding estate was purchased by Councillor Thomas Dormand Stewart (1854–1946) in 1924, who envisaged it as 'a public possession, open and accessible to all the people at all times'. Opened in 1928, Stewart Park remains an important resource for Middlesbrough. Marton Hall was accidentally burned down in 1960, having already been scheduled for demolition. The cause of the fire remained a mystery for over fifty years, until a local resident admitted that her thirteen-year-old brother had started the fire in order to smoke out a pet jackdaw that had flown into the building.

All that survives of Marton Hall is a loggia and several Victorian estate buildings. Essentially a covered external corridor, the loggia was built on the south face of the house *c.* 1860 and gave Bolckow an elegant promenade from which to survey his estate. Retained as a free-standing structure within Stewart Park,

The surviving loggia of Marton Hall (*c.* 1860).

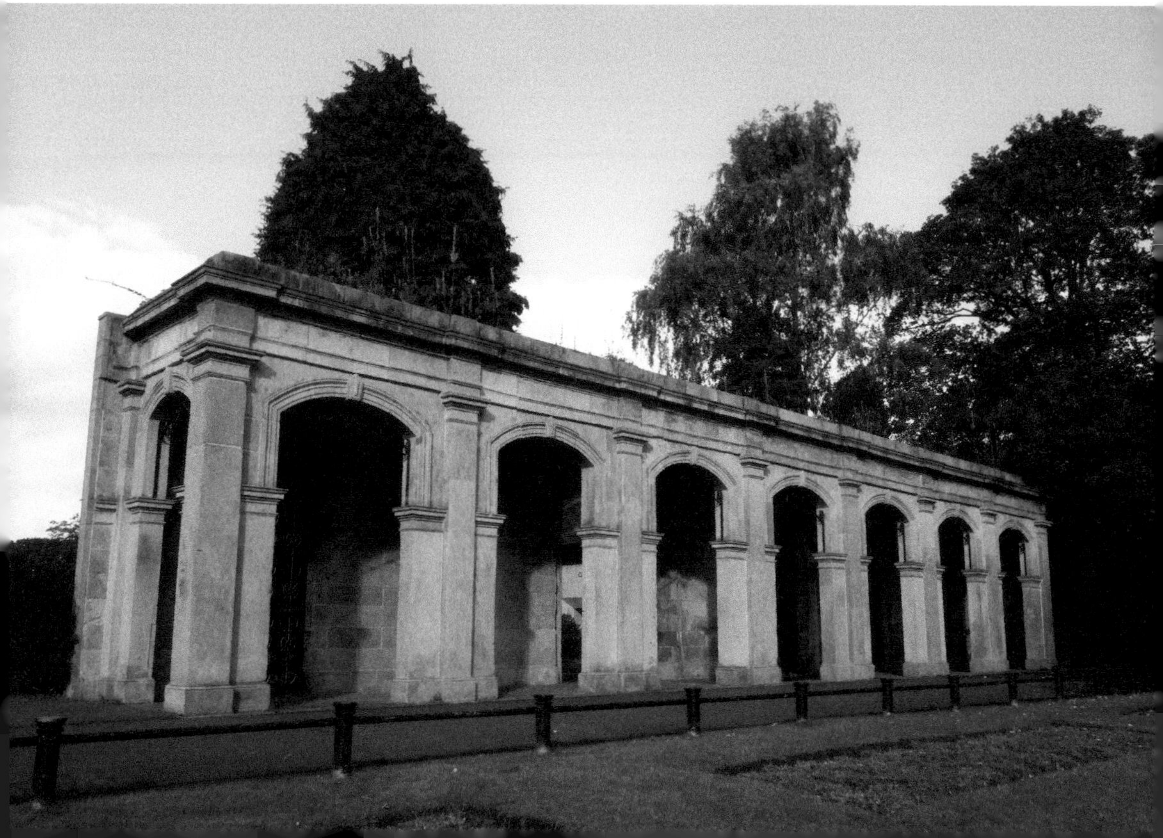

the loggia is built of sandstone in an Italianate style. It consists of segmental arches linked by Tuscan pilasters and surmounted by an entablature. Inside, the floor is lined with flagstones and colourful encaustic tiles.

Bolckow was an avid collector of materials pertaining to James Cook, purchasing his journals, as well as portraits of the explorer. To commemorate Teesside's most famous son, Bolckow erected a memorial on the site of Cook's birthplace in 1858. Consisting of a pink-granite urn on a plinth, it testifies to the civic spirit of the town's great ironmaster, who would himself be immortalised with a monument in 1881.

A mock temple survives as one of several garden buildings erected in the grounds of Marton Hall. Aristocratic patrons of the Georgian era built similar structures in their landscaped gardens to evoke the ancient monuments they had encountered on the Grand Tour. This tradition continued into the Victorian era, when gardens took on further significance as tranquil havens within an increasingly industrialised landscape. This charming folly was built in *c.* 1860 and replicates the small temples built by the Romans for the worship of individual deities. The principal faces are built of dressed sandstone, but cheaper rock-faced stone was used at the rear.

Stewart Park retains the Central Lodge (1864), a multipurpose building incorporating a coach house, stables, laundry and drying room, dairy and lodgings for Bolckow's estate workers. The design reflects the High Victorian Gothic style of *c.* 1850–70, with hard-edged forms and vigorous patterned surfaces made up of red and blue brick and bands of sandstone. Ranged around three sides of a courtyard, the building features east and west lodges and stables which Sir H. G. Reid, founder of the *Middlesbrough Daily Gazette*, described as 'second to none in the north of England'. The steeply pitched roof is clad with fish-scale slates and the gables are augmented with bargeboards and hammer-beams. The Bolckow arms are displayed above the entrance.

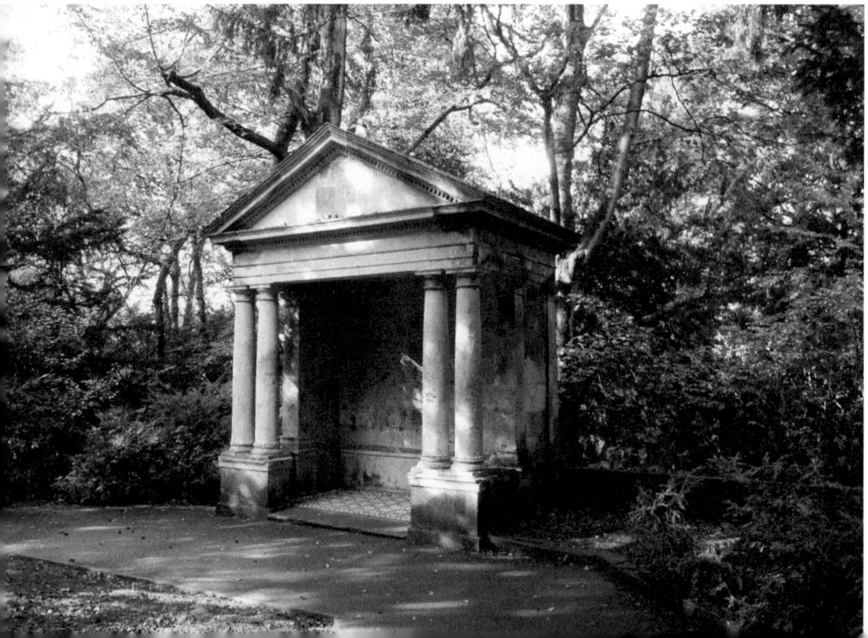

Garden folly in the style of a classical temple (*c.* 1860).

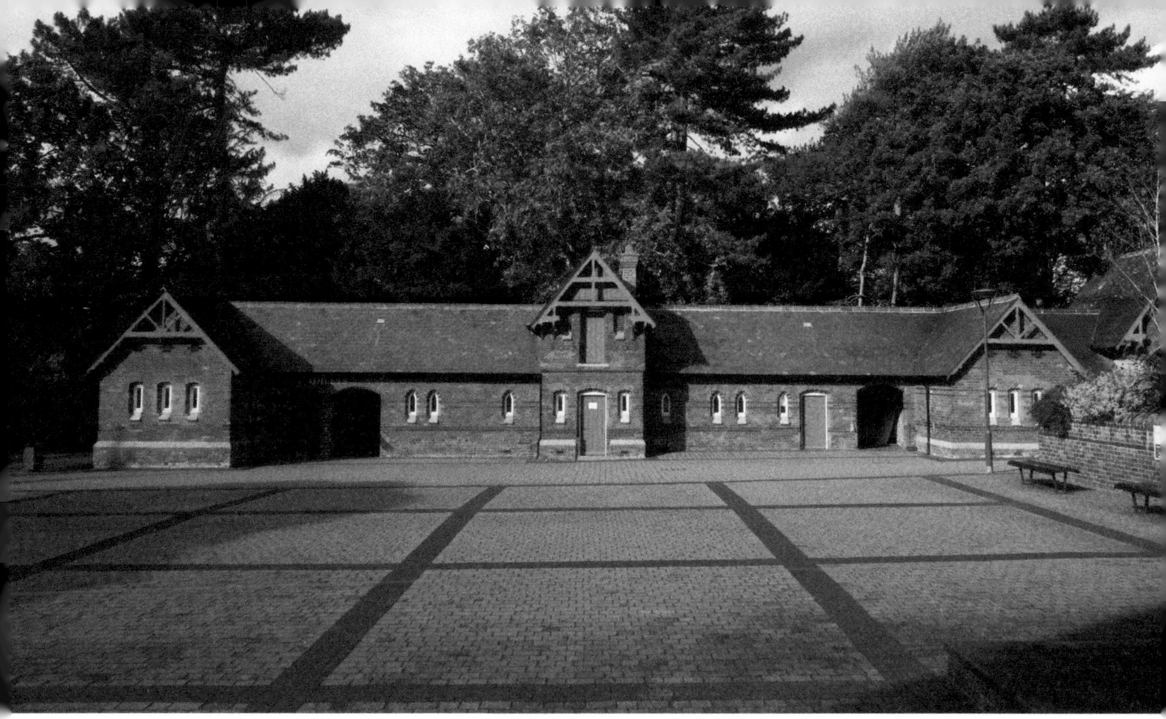

Part of the Central Lodge comprising stables and ancillary buildings (1864).

Zetland Hotel, Zetland Road (1860)

The Zetland Hotel was built around 1860, in a plain expression of the fashionable Italian Renaissance style. Although built of brick, the façade is rendered and scored to resemble stonework. The upper floors, with their regular arrangement of windows, have a pleasing simplicity, accentuated by the jutting Italianate *cornicione* above. The public house frontage to the ground floor incorporates large panes of glass to illuminate the interior. Structural support is provided by square Tuscan columns resting on slender round columns, an inventive but very unusual solution.

No architect has been formally identified, but it is possible that Alfred Waterhouse (1830–1905) was responsible for the design. Cunningham notes that Waterhouse had £7,000 worth of unspecified work at a 'Zetland Hotel' measured by M. Robinson in 1864. The location was unknown at the time of publication, but this record may refer to Middlesbrough's Zetland Hotel.

Stepping inside, the vestibule is graced by a mosaic floor with a Greek key border. The former bar has been refurbished with wood panelling based on surviving fragments of the original. In 1893, John Mitchell Bottomley (1847–1935) extended the building in tune with the late Victorian fashion for spectacular tiled interiors. Bottomley had travelled in Belgium, Italy and France, giving his work an eclectic character. The result was a superb 'luncheon bar' lined with faience tiles and mirrors of etched glass. Executed by Craven Dunnill, the tilework incorporates a wonderous variety of motifs, including waterleaves, shells,

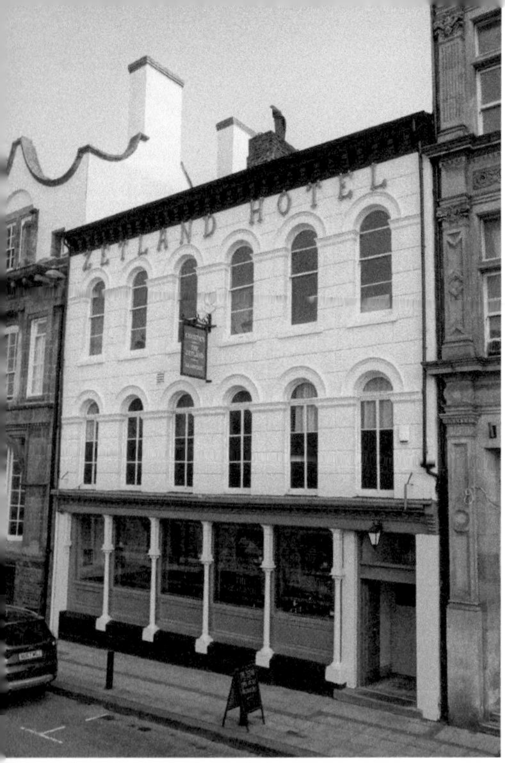

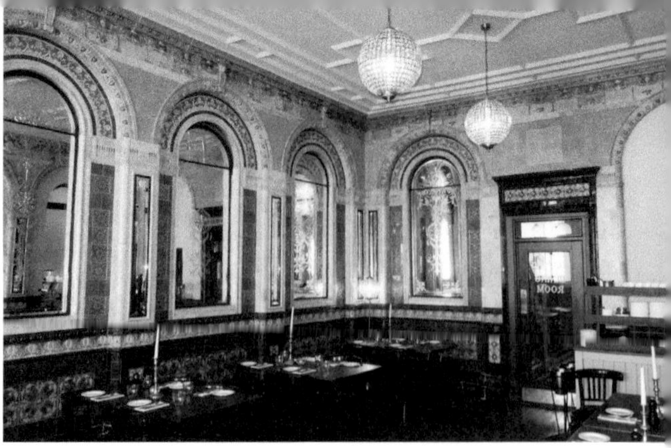

Above: The spectacular tiled interior of the Zetland Hotel.

Left: Zetland Hotel (1860), in a modest Renaissance style.

cherub masks and baskets of fruit. The same firm executed the superb tilework at Waterhouse's Manchester Town Hall (1868–77). Above all this splendour is a lavish Jacobean-style panelled ceiling.

Wesley Central Mission, Linthorpe Road (1860–63)

The Wesley Central Mission was the largest Nonconformist chapel in Middlesbrough, a colossal edifice standing at the junction of Linthorpe and Corporation Roads. Better known as 'Big Wesley', this giant chapel was able to seat as many as 840 worshippers. The imposing design was modelled on the great churches of the Renaissance, themselves adaptations of Greco-Roman temples. The use of a classical aesthetic defined the building as a Dissenting chapel, in contrast to the Gothic churches of the Anglican faith.

In essence, the chapel was a gargantuan preaching hall with towering walls of brick and stone laid in complex rhythmic patterns. The façades were arrayed with giant pilasters and round-headed arches, intensifying the effect. The result was a dazzling display of 'structural polychromy', in which colour is built into the fabric of buildings through the use of multicoloured materials. The ironmaster John Vaughan contributed £1,200 towards the building cost of £6,000. Schools were added in 1865 at a cost of £2,000. Big Wesley closed its doors in 1953, when the congregation moved to the Park Methodist Chapel on Linthorpe Road. Tragically, the building was demolished in September 1955 to make way for a branch of British Home Stores (1958), depriving Middlesbrough of an extraordinary building.

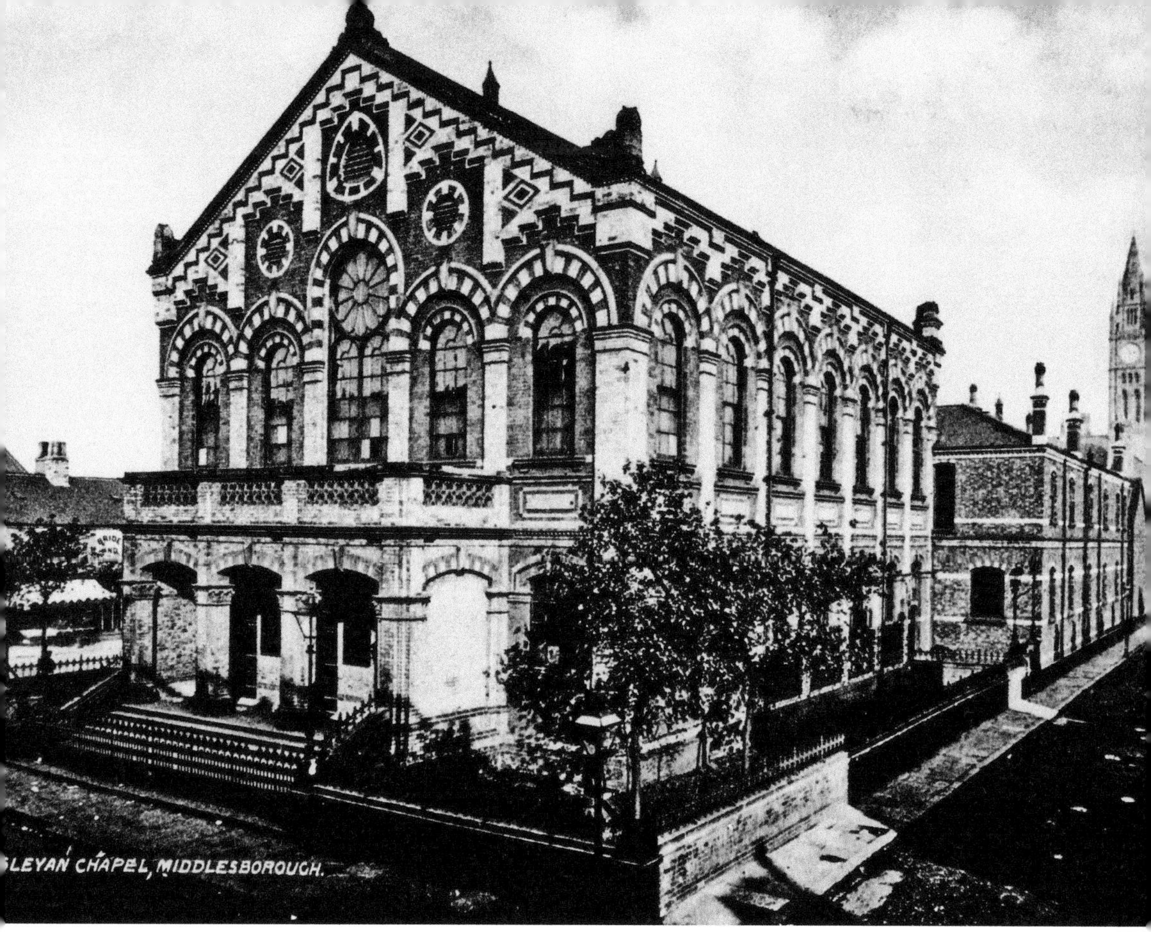

Wesley Central Mission, known as 'Big Wesley' (1860–63). (Middlesbrough Libraries and Information)

North Riding Infirmary, Hartington Road (1860–64)

Under the leadership of Henry Bolckow, the Middlesbrough ironmasters decided to build a hospital for those who 'might need surgical aid through accidents at the different ironworks and mines'. In 1859, Thomas Hustler (1801–74) of Acklam Hall offered an acre of land on the Long Plantation between Newport Road and what became Parliament Road. The family also offered a subscription of £80, while Bolckow promised £5,000 towards the final cost of £7,865.

The North Riding Infirmary was designed by Oliver and Lamb of Newcastle in a graceful Italianate style. The layout was based on domestic plans developed by Renaissance architect Andrea Palladio (1508–80), comprising a central administration block and two pavilion wards, connected by low ranges. This arrangement helped to prevent the spread of infectious diseases, while still providing efficient circulation for staff.

The building continued to evolve as ever greater demands were made on the infirmary. New operating theatres, wards and a reception room opened in 1896.

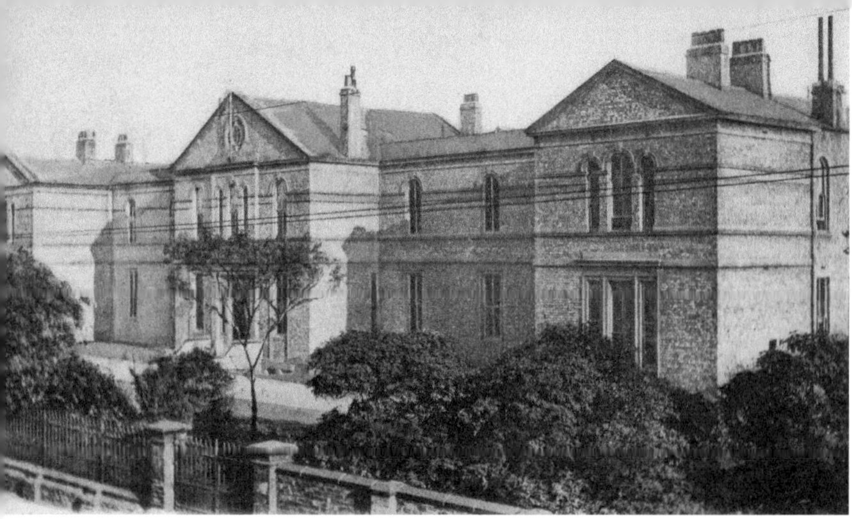

The former North Riding Infirmary (1860–64). (Middlesbrough Libraries and Information)

Queen Victoria's Diamond Jubilee in 1897 gave the necessary impetus to build a children's ward with nurses' sitting room and bedrooms above. Following the death of Sir Bernhard Samuelson, his family funded the building of a memorial wing in his honour (1907).

The infirmary treated injuries sustained by industrial workers until it became an ear, nose and throat hospital. In 2006, the regrettable decision was taken to demolish this fine Victorian building and replace it with a supermarket of banal design, despite strong public opposition. The only part to survive is the building's splendid baroque portico, which has been reconstructed off Hartington Road.

St John the Evangelist's Church, Marton Road (1863–65)

St John's Church is the finest example of High Victorian Gothic architecture in Middlesbrough. With its muscular form, hard edges and polychrome surfaces, it exemplifies the neo-medieval style developed for the large urban churches of industrial Britain. The church was designed by John Norton (1823–1904) of Bristol and London, formerly a friend of Pugin, along with a school and parsonage to the south. Jonas France of Middlesbrough was the contractor and the aptly named Mr Sturdy acted as clerk of works. The foundation stone was laid on 11 November 1863 on land given by A. B. Cochrane. Construction cost £4,000, exclusive of the tower and spire, which brought the total to £5,500.

The vast bulk comprises a nave with aisles, clerestory and fully formed transepts, all executed in the Early English Gothic style of the thirteenth century. The simple lancet windows contain plate tracery, the earliest form of Gothic tracery, in which the openings give the appearance of having been cut into flat plates of masonry. Illustrating the eclectic nature of Victorian architecture, the chancel ends with a splendid polygonal apse derived from French sources and braced with immense buttresses. Echoing the work of George Edmund Street (1824–81) and William Butterfield (1814–1900), the church is built of red brick, but relieved by bands, diapering and ornamental patterns of blue brick and stone. This is perhaps the most impressive example of 'structural polychromy' in Middlesbrough.

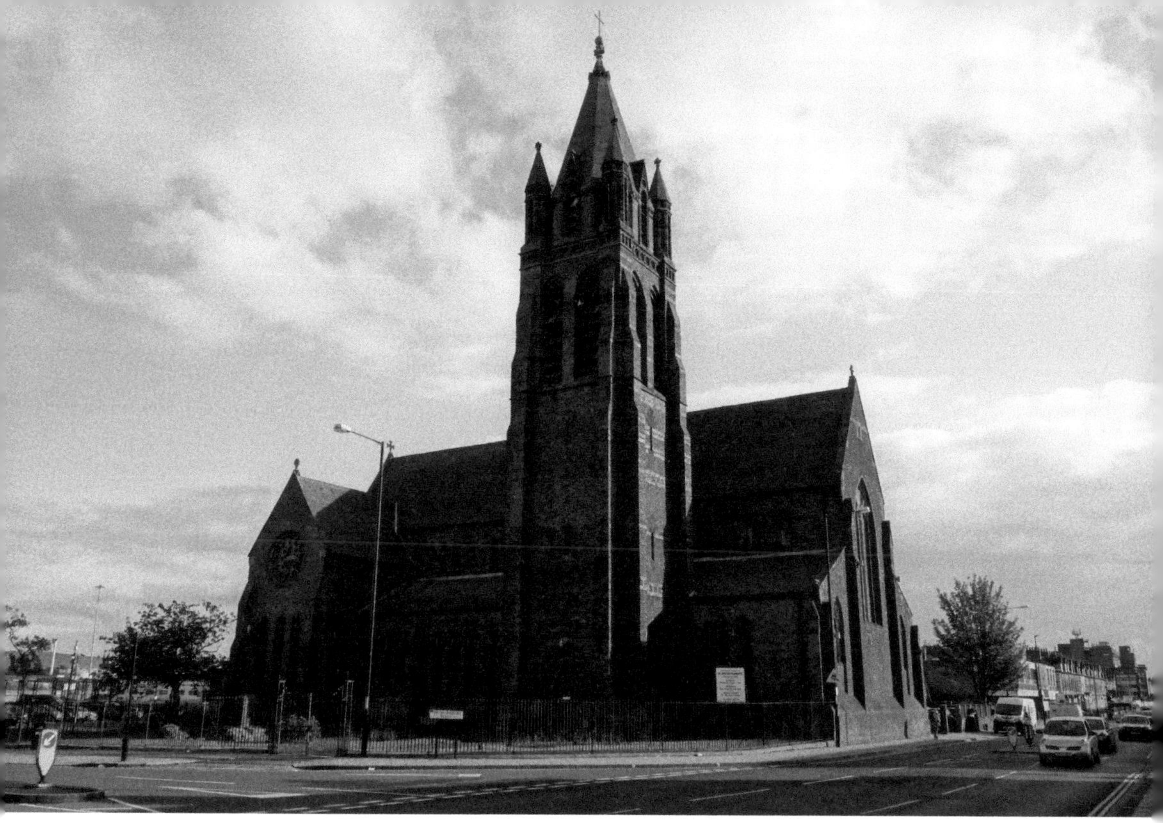

St John the Evangelist's Church (1863–65), a monument of High Victorian Gothic.

Norton's original design included a tower with soaring broach spire, but this was not built during the first phase of construction. Oliver and Johnson of Newcastle were subsequently contracted to design a spire, but this too was abandoned. The present spire was built in 1881–83 to designs by local architects John William Alexander (*fl.* 1876–91) and William Henman (1846–1917). The spire is much shorter than that proposed by Norton, but the result is impressively robust.

Designed to accommodate 900 worshippers, the spacious interior exhibits the same vibrant colour as the exterior. Round piers support sharply pointed arches. The stone carving, font, pulpit and original reredos were all executed by William Farmer (1825–79) of London, who founded the renowned firm of architectural sculptors Farmer & Brindley. The church was extended at the west end by C. G. Hare of London in 1914, as is apparent from the discontinuation of the polychrome brickwork. The original west window was retained, displaying flowing Decorated-style tracery. The demolition of St Hilda's Church in the 1960s made St John's the oldest church in central Middlesbrough.

Royal Exchange, Exchange Place (1865–68)

The Royal Exchange was the commercial heart of Middlesbrough, providing a palatial venue for the trading of iron, the lifeblood of the town. The new building stood at the centre of Exchange Place, close to the railway station, which provided a vital artery for the transportation of goods. A statement of Victorian grandiloquence, the building was designed by Charles John Adams (1838/9–79) of Stockton, whose plans were placed on public view in the Town Hall in January 1865, where they could be viewed for one shilling. Inspiration came from the town palaces erected by the powerful merchants of the Italian Renaissance, who can be seen as the antecedents of the Victorian capitalist class. Symbolising commercial enterprise, the Renaissance style was used for many of the buildings erected around Exchange Place.

The foundation stone was laid by Henry Bolckow, chairman of the Middlesbrough Exchange Company, on 22 November 1866. Construction cost £28,000, but as funds ran out, plans to erect a 130-foot tower had to be abandoned. At each corner stood a monumental pavilion, giving the building a commanding presence. The lower windows featured keystones sculpted with the faces of Roman gods, here taking on the allegorical connotation of industrial titans. Linking the pavilions were towering brick walls, pierced by arcades and round-headed windows. Uncharacteristically for an Italianate building, the roofline was richly ornamented with chimney stacks and Mansard roofs.

The Exchange opened for business on 29 July 1868. Inside was a vast hall measuring 160 feet by 60 feet with a vaulted ceiling. Flanking the hall were two tiers of offices. Dining rooms, a licensed restaurant and cellars were provided, as well as accommodation for the Cleveland Club of manufacturers, merchants and professional men. When Middlesbrough's Iron Age came to an end, the building

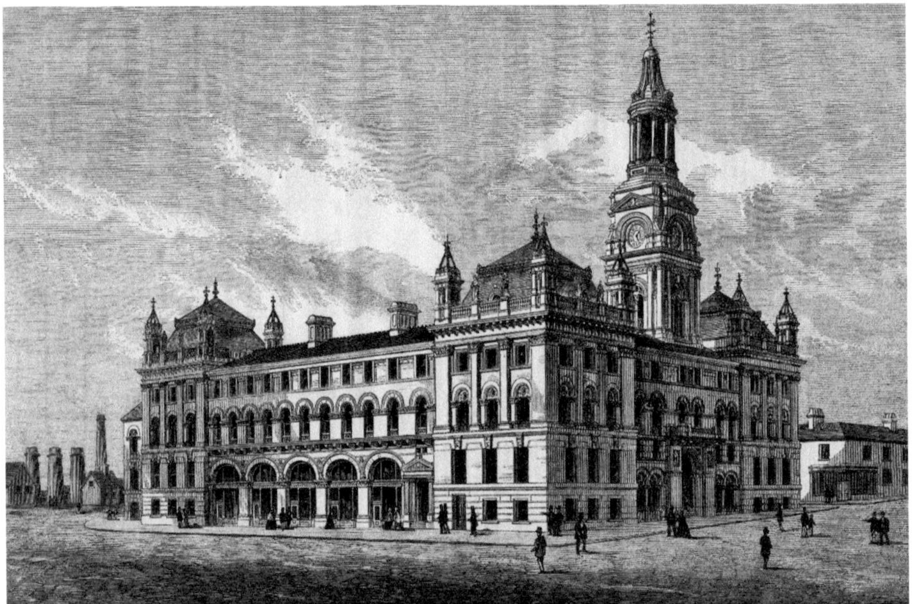

The Royal Exchange as published in *The Builder* (1868), showing the proposed tower.

fell into disuse. It was eventually demolished in 1985 to make way for the A66 motorway. A dour concrete flyover now cuts through this historic quarter, casting a dystopian atmosphere over the noble buildings of a former age. This surely ranks as the worst planning decision in Middlesbrough's history. Salvaged keystones from the Exchange were recontextualised as street ornaments, but only serve to emphasise what has been lost.

Holy Trinity, Market Place, North Ormesby (1868–69)

Holy Trinity is yet another striking church, located in North Ormesby, a suburb of Middlesbrough that was laid out *c.* 1860. The church was designed by William White, but extended by Armfield and Bottomley in 1879, with further alterations in 1925 and 1929. In the angular plan and use of cheap brick, it anticipates Temple Moore's extraordinary church of St Columba, but the soaring tower makes it distinctive, emphasised by tapering buttresses that rise all the way to the summit. The tower is pierced by concentric brick arches, forming stark, gaping portals and the structure is capped with stout polygonal piers at the corners. Overall, the building gives the impression of honest construction and powerful forms. The brick execution complements the surrounding urban landscape of terraced housing, defining this as a church of the people.

Holy Trinity Church, North Ormesby (1868–69), displaying its striking tower.

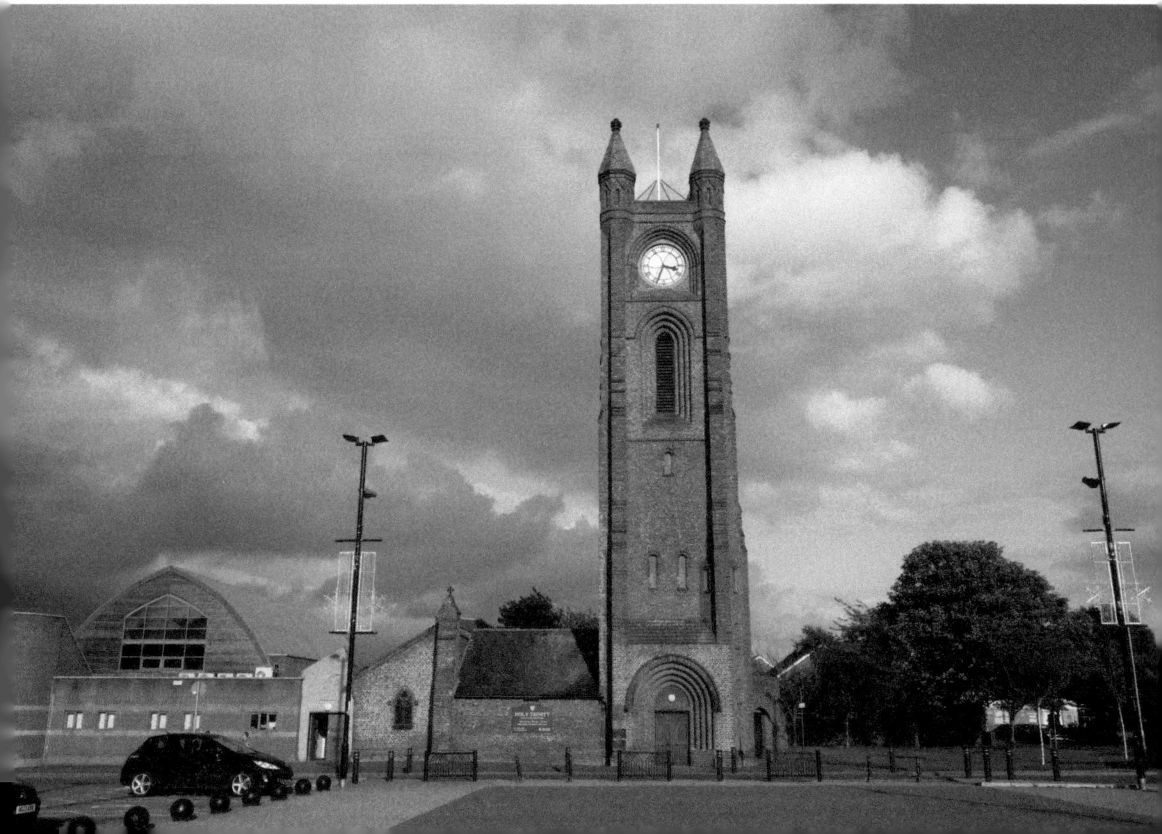

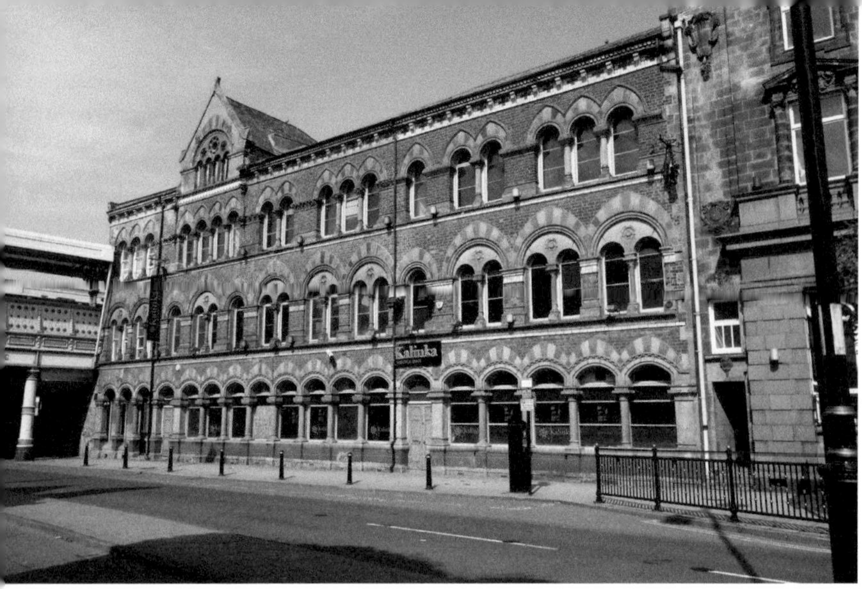

Albert Bridge Place (1870), evoking an Italian Gothic *palazzo*.

Albert Bridge Place, Exchange Place (1870)

This Victorian office block, formerly known as Albert Bridge Place, was designed in the Italian Gothic style popularised by John Ruskin's influential publication *The Stones of Venice* (1851–53). Victorian architects scoured history for inspiration to help them design the new building types required by an industrial capitalist society. For multi-storey office buildings, the *palazzi* or town palaces of the Italian Renaissance provided an appropriate model, enabling architects to combine public shops on the ground floor with private offices above, all enclosed behind a dignified façade. Alluding to powerful mercantile dynasties such as the Medici, the *palazzo* model was a suitable idiom for the new palaces of Victorian capitalism.

Albert Bridge Place was designed by W. H. Blessley and presents a vigorous façade in polychrome brick and stone. Emulating precedents such as the Palazzo Ducale in Mantua, an arcade spans the ground floor and the upper storeys have varied fenestration. The windows are separated by granite colonettes, or slender columns, and framed by Venetian Gothic arches. With its powerful chromatic effect, enhanced by a band of encaustic tiles, the design anticipates Blessley's later Zetland Buildings just around the corner.

St Paul's Church, Newport Road (1870–71)

St Paul's Church was built on land donated by the Hustler family of Acklam Hall. It was known as the church of Middlesbrough's iron and steel industry, as its construction was funded by local firms and their workers. The design was well adapted to its industrial setting. With its hard, angular forms and polychrome brick surfaces, it exemplified the 'muscular Gothic' style developed for urban churches in the High Victorian period. St Paul's was designed by the talented

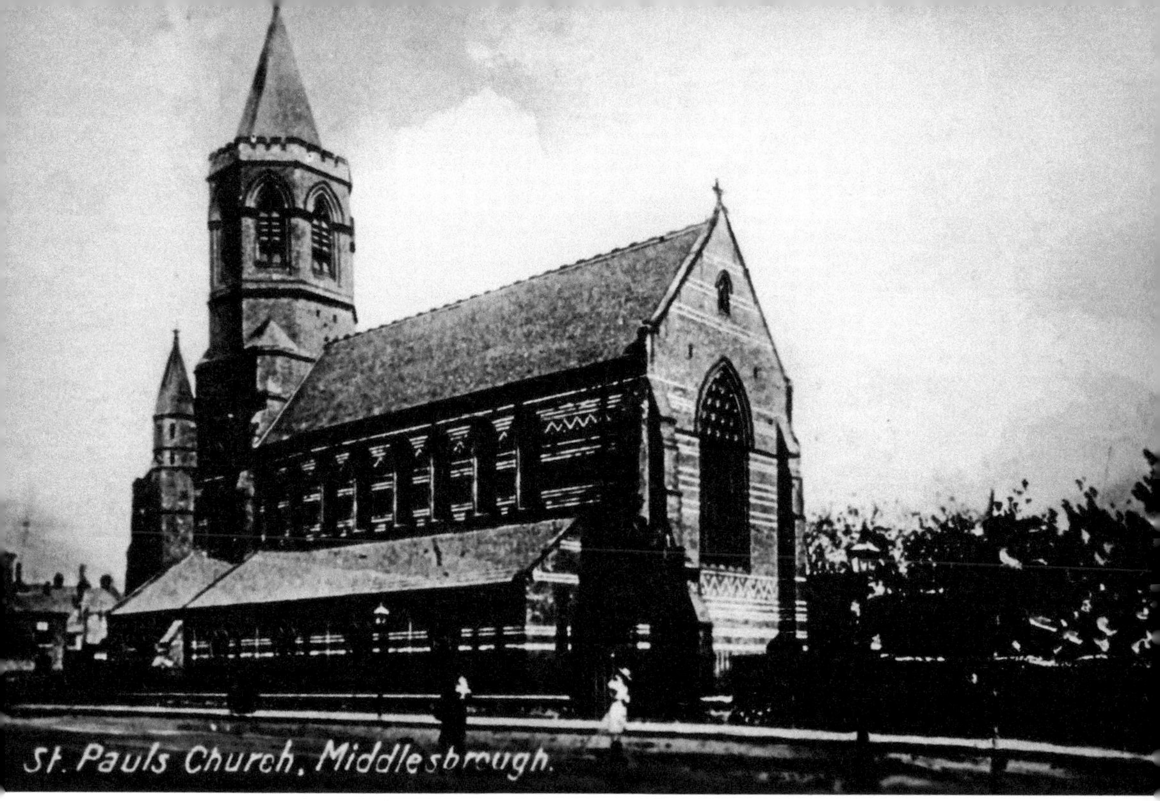

Above: St Paul's Church (1870–71), exemplifying the brilliance of R. J. Johnson.

Right: Interior of St Paul's Church. (Middlesbrough Libraries and Information)

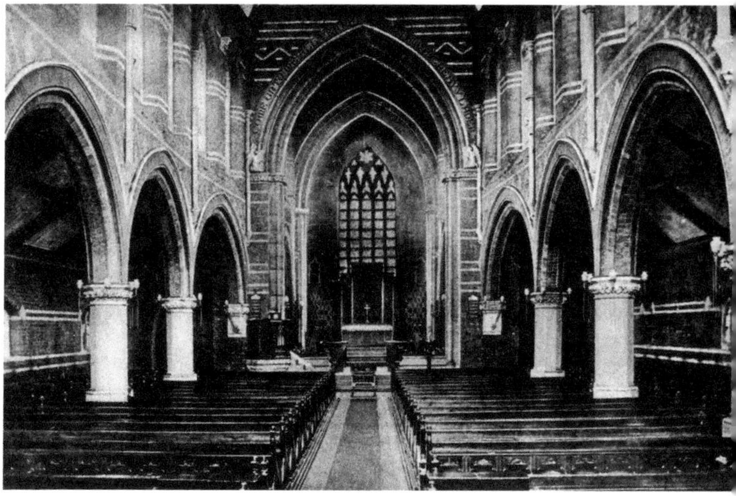

and highly versatile architect Robert James Johnson (1832–92) of Newcastle. Born in Stokesley, North Yorkshire, Johnson undertook several commissions in Middlesbrough.

St Paul's was a church of soaring proportions thanks to an extremely tall clerestory pierced by simple lancet windows. The building's east and west faces were sheer expanses of dark red brick, reinforced with immense buttresses. Crowning the structure was a robust octagonal tower, arrayed with battlements, and a tall spire. These were placed over the junction between nave and chancel, giving the east end a powerful vertical emphasis.

No less impressive was the interior, where the nave arcades and clerestory were executed in red brick, with bands and zigzags of yellow brick to create visual interest. A lofty chancel arch framed the view of the altar and across it was written the Biblical verse 'Come unto me all ye that labour and are heavy laden,' words that held great significance for the working people of Middlesbrough. Tragically, the church was damaged by bombing in 1941 and was eventually demolished in 1967. The site is now occupied by a modern housing development.

Printing Works and Offices, Zetland Road (1865–71 and 1888–93)

The architecture of Zetland Road is enhanced by these late Victorian commercial buildings, which were commissioned by Sir H. G. Reid as printing works and offices for the *North Eastern Daily Gazette*, Middlesbrough's first daily newspaper. No. 13 was built in 1865–71 to designs by W. H. Blessley. The premises were extended with the building of No. 11 in 1888–93 by Roger Lofthouse (1845–1901). Both were built of brick and faced with sandstone to project an image of sophistication and prosperity.

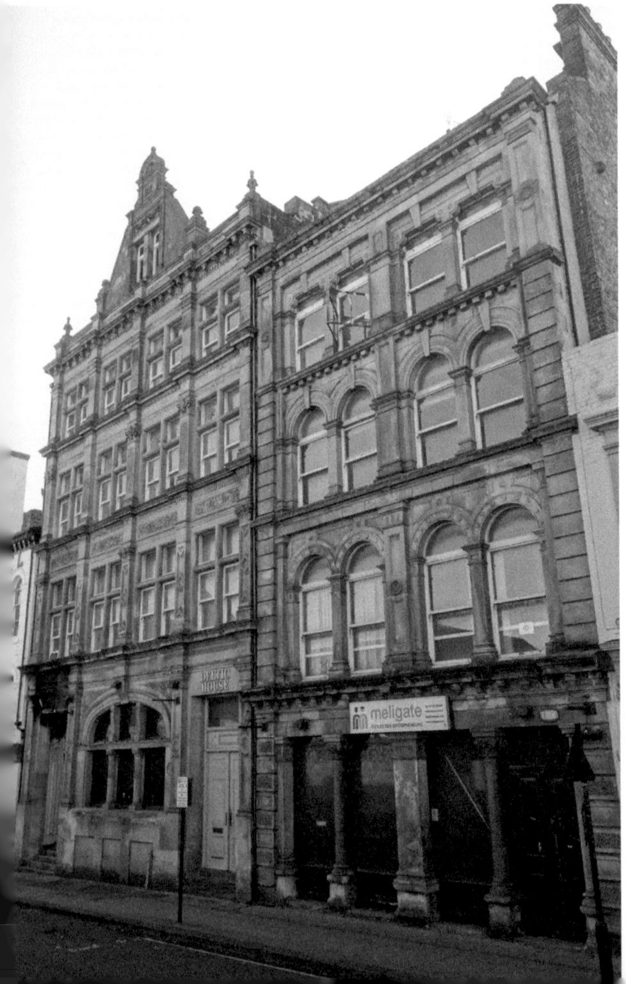

Printing Works and Offices (1865–71 and 1888–93).

The earlier of the two buildings reflects the Italian Renaissance style that was fashionable in the 1860s. Like many commercial buildings of the era, it was based on the town palaces of the Italian Renaissance. Not only did this model provide an excellent basis for designing multi-storey buildings, it allowed Victorian capitalists to portray themselves as successors to the great mercantile dynasties of the past. The ground floor is treated as a shopfront, with large areas of glazing and columns to support the upper floors. The principal floors feature Renaissance-style windows and rusticated quoins to convey an impression of strength.

By the time the property was extended in 1888, architectural tastes had shifted. No. 11 was designed in a Northern Renaissance style, alluding to the wealthy mercantile culture that flourished in Belgium, Flanders and the Netherlands between the fifteenth and seventeenth centuries. Like the Italian Renaissance style, this served as a flattering metaphor for Victorian trade and commerce. The building is taller than its neighbour and features a grid-like façade divided by enriched pilasters and horizontal stringcourses. There is much fine carving in the form of dated escutcheons, a decorative frieze of foliated scrolls and a parapet with ball finials. The design culminates in a shaped gable with 'acroteria', architectural ornaments mounted at the apex and corners of a pediment.

Zetland Buildings, Exchange Square (1872)

The undulating façade of the Zetland Buildings defined the northern perimeter of Exchange Place, the commercial district surrounding Middlesbrough's Royal Exchange. Constructed in three stages from designs by W. H. Blessley, the building provided offices for various businesses and formed an almost theatrical backdrop for one of Middlesbrough's major civic spaces. With its vibrant colour effects and stratified composition, the building recalls Blessley's slightly earlier design for Albert Bridge Place (1870). However, the Zetland Buildings were designed on a larger scale in the form of a sweeping terrace.

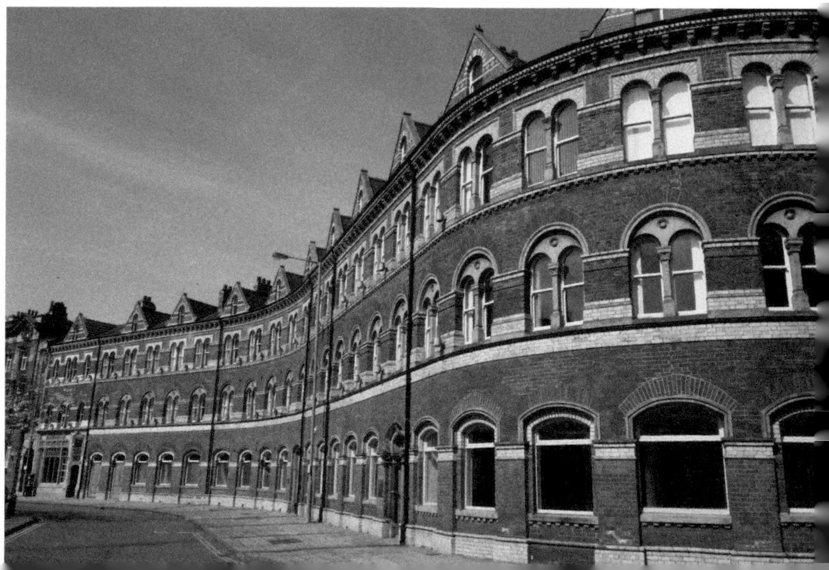

The sweeping façade of the Zetland Buildings (1872).

The use of buttresses and bracketed eaves gives variation and depth to the façade, while the rhythm created by the paired windows and gabled dormers is highly inventive. The most conspicuous feature, however, is the bold curve as the building runs around the corner into Zetland Place. With the demolition of the Royal Exchange for the ruthless insertion of the A66 flyover, Exchange Place was transformed into an open public square. Despite its catastrophic impact on Middlesbrough's heritage, this decision has opened up a grand panorama, and the processional effect of the surviving buildings makes a powerful architectural statement.

Commerce House, Exchange Square (1872)

Commerce House is part of the Zetland Buildings, an extraordinary architectural showpiece that was built in three stages from 1872 to provide offices for letting, all screened by a multicoloured Italian-style façade. In 1885, the westernmost property was acquired by the North Eastern Banking Co. and the ground floor was remodelled by William Lister Newcombe (1857–1929) and William Henry Knowles (1847–1943) of Newcastle.

The ground floor was clad in Jacobethan-style ornament consisting of intricate panels filled with carved foliage. Knowles was a noted antiquarian and his design work frequently drew upon his deep knowledge of historic buildings. The door sits

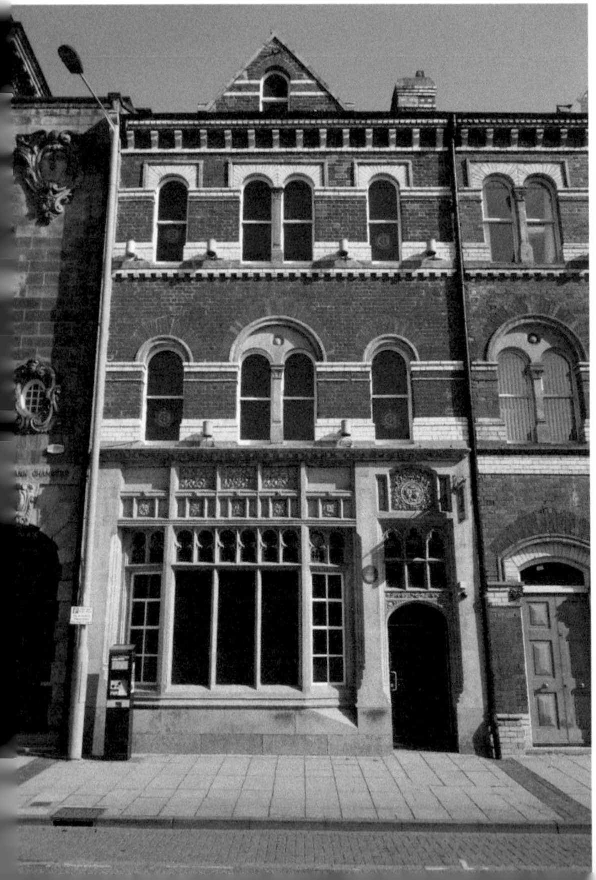

Commerce House (1872), remodelled in Jacobethan style.

within a shallow Tudor-Gothic arch, enriched with further carved foliage and a roundel displaying the arms of Middlesbrough and Newcastle, where the bank was established in 1872 to provide finance for heavy industry. All this work was executed in sandstone and displays exceptional craftsmanship. Currently known as Bolckow House, the building is used as offices for the North East Chamber of Commerce.

National Provincial Bank, Cleveland Street (1870–72)

Middlesbrough's industrial enterprises required a substantial banking infrastructure in order to maintain ready reserves of capital. A branch of the National Provincial Bank was built on a site previously occupied by the house of John Gilbert Holmes, one of Middlesbrough's first shipbuilders. The National Provincial was one of the first banking corporations in Britain to establish a nationwide branch network. The building was designed by the firm's architect John Gibson (1817–92) of Westminster, thus introducing a note of metropolitan sophistication to Middlesbrough's architecture.

Most of the firm's buildings occupy prestigious corner sites, but the Middlesbrough branch occupies a fully detached island site, making it all the more imposing. As a former assistant to Sir Charles Barry (1795–1860), Gibson generally favoured the classical and Renaissance styles in his designs. However, the Middlesbrough building exhibits a richer French baroque style. Victorian banks typically used architecture to portray themselves as stable and prosperous institutions and this building is no exception. The imposing single-storey block is encased in heavy ornamentation, which conveys both richness and strength. The central door is framed by a bold portico with a magnificent sculpted pediment. Within the tympanum are allegorical figures of Britannia, an ironworker

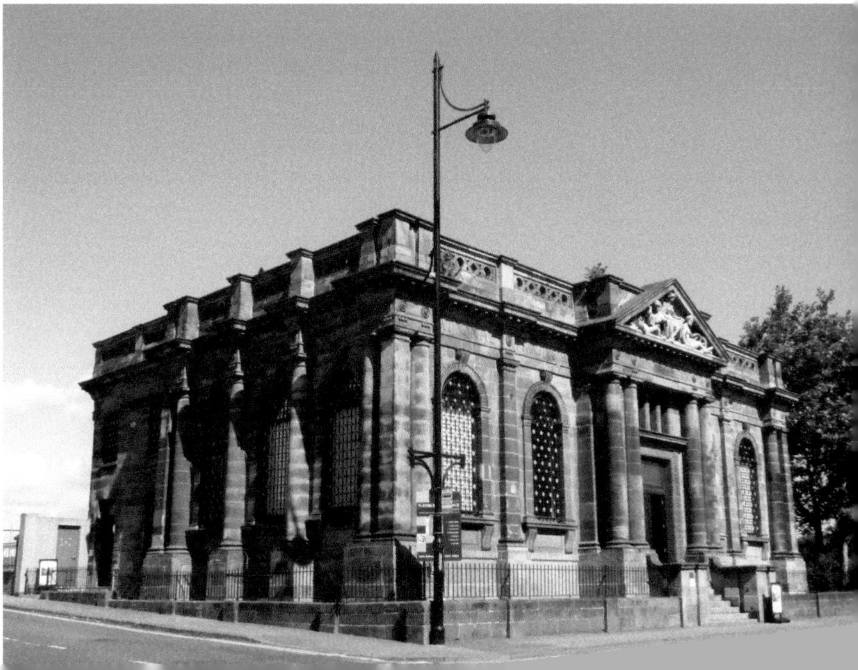

National Provincial Bank (1870–72), by John Gibson.

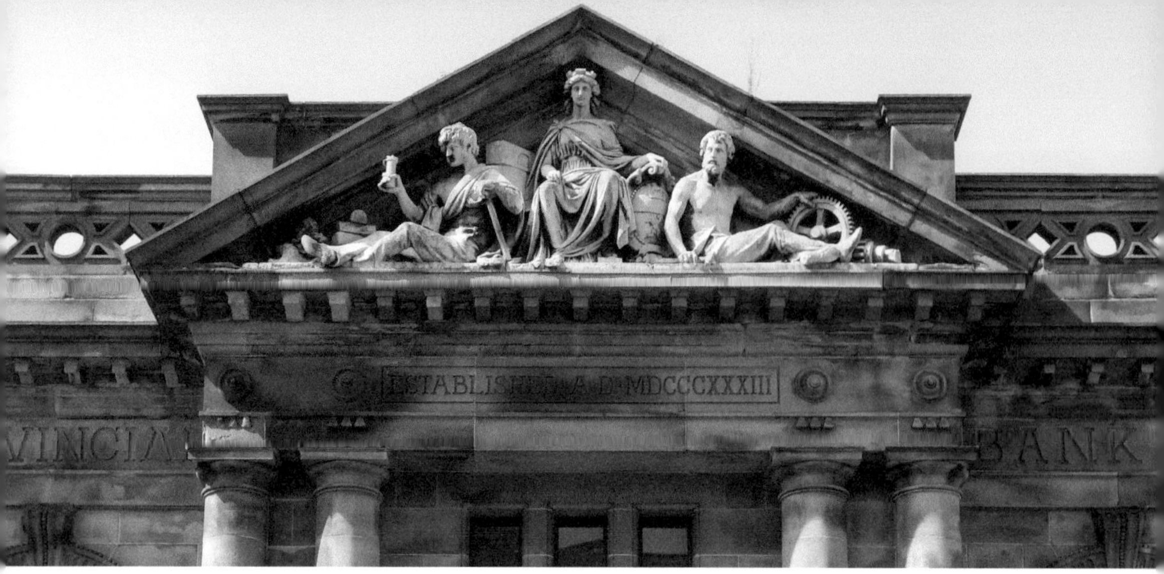

Allegorical figures within the lavish pediment.

and a miner, symbolising the industries that generated Middlesbrough's wealth. These were sculpted by Charles Henry Mabey (*c.* 1836–1912) of London.

The façade is punctuated by round-headed windows with Tuscan surrounds. These were typical of Gibson's work and reveal his affinity for Renaissance architecture. The windows have iron grilles to assure investors that their money was protected, although these are not the originals. Likewise, the large doors are later additions. As in all of Gibson's branches for the National Provincial Bank, the entablature is inscribed with the company's name and date of establishment. A heavy cornice crowns the building, beneath a parapet pierced with geometric ornamentation. Converted to a private clubhouse in 1936, the building became a meeting place for the Cleveland Club.

Jonathan Backhouse and Co. Bank, Albert Road (1872–73)

This neo-Gothic palace on Albert Road was the Middlesbrough branch of the Backhouse and Company Bank, which was founded in 1774. The firm's flagship premises at Darlington were designed by Alfred Waterhouse in 1864–67. His initial sketches show a High Renaissance design much as Sir Charles Barry or John Gibson might have produced, but he later adapted this into a Gothic design with the same basic plan and fenestration. This change in style suggests a degree of uncertainty on the part of the client. Once Backhouse had accepted the Gothic style, however, it was maintained in other branches.

The Middlesbrough branch of this 'old and deservedly respected firm' was designed by George Gordon Hoskins (1836/7–1911) of Darlington, who was well qualified for the task. Hoskins had served as Waterhouse's clerk of works for Pilmore Hall at Hurworth, County Durham (1861–64). He was also clerk of works at the Darlington branch of Backhouse Bank and designed the manager's

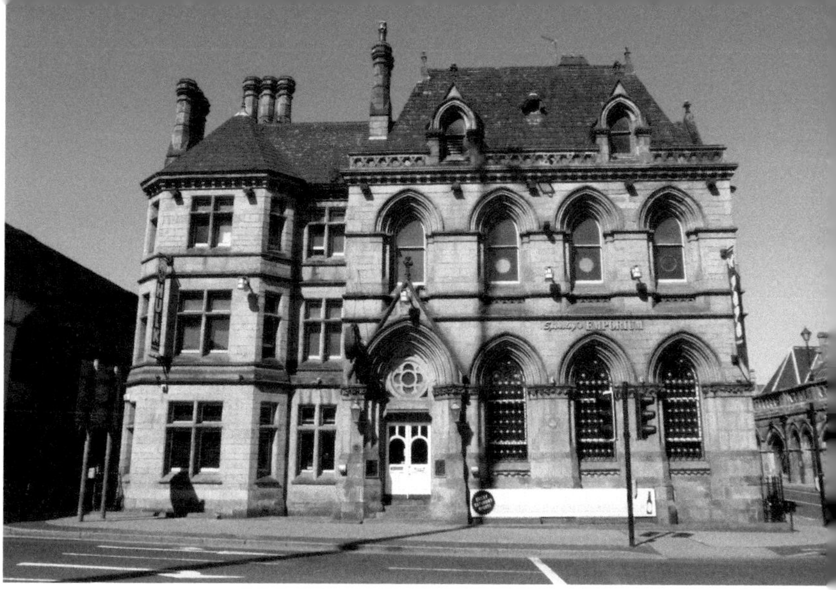

Jonathan Backhouse and Co. Bank and manager's house (1872–73).

house in 1867. As a result, Hoskins was able to continue Waterhouse's style in his own branches for Sunderland (1868), Bishop Auckland (1871) and Middlesbrough. When a competition was held to obtain designs for Middlesbrough's new Town Hall in 1883, it was Waterhouse who awarded first prize to Hoskins' design, which used the same style as the Middlesbrough bank, though on a grander scale.

The bank was designed in a French Gothic style typical of the High Victorian period (*c.* 1850–70), when architects began to embrace Continental influences. French Gothic architecture is characterised by massiveness and strength, qualities that were ideal for a bank building, which needed to instil confidence into its customers. To convey a sense of impregnability, the walls are immensely thick at the base, chamfered to form a rugged plinth and strong buttresses between the windows.

The main entrance is set within a deeply moulded Gothic canopy with a quatrefoil window overhead. The lower windows are covered with ornamental wrought-iron grilles made by Siddell of Darlington, giving the effect of a fortified building. The upper windows are set within Gothic arches, but the usual tracery has been omitted in order to provide good light for the first-floor offices. French pavilion roofs give the building a distinctive profile, accentuated by niche-like dormer windows. A bank manager's house was built alongside the main building in a complementary, but more domestic style.

The entire edifice was built by Messrs Dennett of London and Nottingham using fireproof construction. Charles Colton Dennett patented a method of fireproof construction in 1857 and a slightly revised method in 1863. His system consisted of concrete arches supported at intermediate points by iron girders. The concrete was made of broken stone embedded in calcined gypsum plaster rather than cement. Hoskins used this system in several projects, including Middlesbrough Town Hall.

Sadly, the interior has been altered, but enough detail survives to give an impression of what must have been an imposing banking hall. A fine panelled ceiling and cornice remain. The interior was described as being 'somewhat unique in treatment', in that the public and cashiers' areas were separated by an arcade of Gothic arches, a system Hoskins had previously used at the Sunderland branch. Besides delineating the space, the arcade was intended to meet some of the requirements of the fireproof construction. The floor above the banking hall was devoted to a 'lofty and commodious' suite of offices. These had an independent entrance and, by judicious arrangement of plan, did not interfere with the bank portion.

Various firms contributed to the building. Jackson of Middlesbrough carried out the brickwork and masonry, while the architectural carving was executed by the respected firm of Farmer & Brindley of London, who worked on many of Waterhouse's buildings, including the Natural History Museum in London (1873–80). George Pattison of Darlington provided the slate roof. Internally, Maw and Co. provided tiled flooring, while R. M. Ormerod of Carlisle did the plastering and Hudson of Middlesbrough the plumbing and glazing. All of the carpentry was executed by R. Robson and Son of Durham. For security, the bank required strongroom doors and safes, and these were supplied by Chubb.

All Saints' Church, Linthorpe Road (1873–78)

With Middlesbrough's population growing rapidly, a new church was needed to alleviate the overburdened parishes of St John and St Paul. A new parish was formed in 1871 and named All Saints by the Archbishop of York, who secured the site from the Middlesbrough Owners for £3,300. Subscriptions of £4,000 were obtained, mostly from the town's ironmasters. In December 1873, a tender of £7,774 from the builders Simpson and Baker of London was accepted.

All Saints' Church was designed by George Edmund Street, the prominent Victorian architect best known for his majestic design for the Royal Courts of Justice in London (1873-82). Street was among the leading exponents of the Gothic Revival and a man at the forefront of his profession. All Saints' is a relatively modest design for an industrial town, but it nevertheless displays Street's skill in neo-medieval design.

The exterior is designed in the Decorated style, a phase of English Gothic architecture that flourished *c.* 1280–1380, but the interior reveals a strong influence from Italian Gothic churches. The influential Ecclesiological Society, of which Street was a member, had viewed Decorated Gothic as the zenith of medieval architecture. By the 1870s, however, the Society was beginning to release church architects from strict copyism of English forms and was encouraging the use of foreign details.

The bulk is executed in rock-faced limestone with ashlar dressings, producing a rich textural contrast. The plan is essentially rectangular, but Street was able to convey a cruciform effect by introducing eastern transepts that rise above the aisles. The composition of the west front is distinctive. A projecting porch houses a door, deeply recessed under moulded arches. Strong buttresses flanking the porch

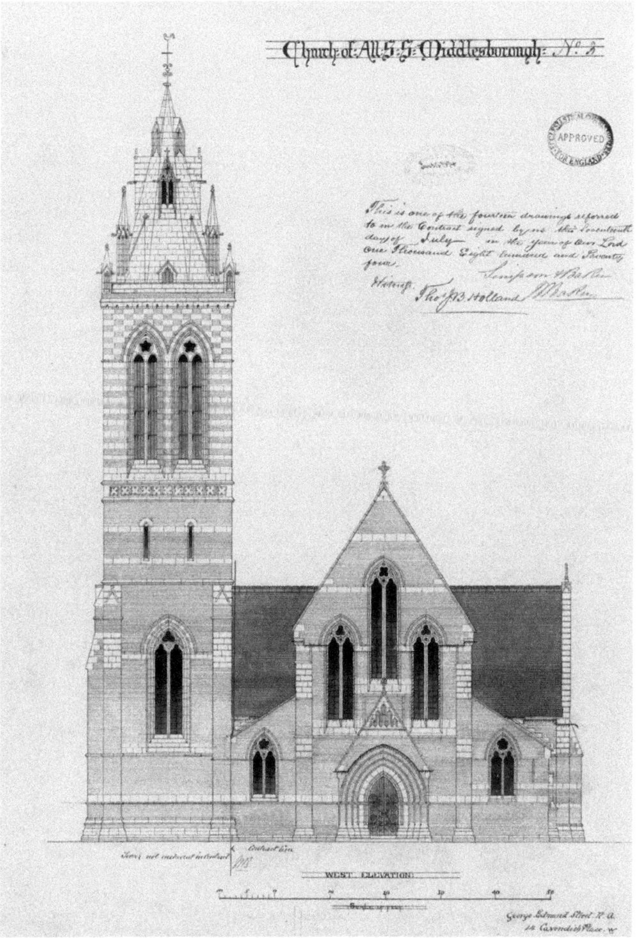

G. E. Street's design for All Saints' Church (1873–78), showing the proposed tower. (RIBA Collections)

contribute a sense of solidity. Street intended to erect a tower at the north-west corner, but this was never built due to a shortage of funds. There is, however, an octagonal sanctus bell turret rising from the north transept.

As with many of Street's churches, the interior is lined with polychrome brickwork, a feature inspired by his study of Italian Gothic architecture. Street published an influential book on this subject in 1855, entitled *Brick and Marble in the Middle Ages: notes of a tour in the north of Italy*. The brick walls contrast with fine stone arcades which lead the eye to the focal point of the interior, an alabaster tabernacle arrayed with buttresses, a portcullis and battlements. Behind this is a reredos (1891) by Burlison and Grylls, featuring traceried panels and images of the Evangelists and prophets. The same firm produced the stained glass in the eastern rose window (1890), which depicts Christ the King.

The chief glory of the interior is the stained glass by Morris, Marshall, Faulkner & Co. William Morris (1834–96) had trained in Street's office, with the intention of becoming an architect, but he later abandoned this ambition and channelled his talents into the decorative arts and writing. He co-founded Morris & Co. in 1861, the most important firm associated with the Arts and Crafts movement. The firm created the St Aidan and St Boniface window (1889), based on cartoons by Edward Burne-Jones, who also designed the St Alban window (1864).

St Mary's Cathedral, Sussex Street (1876–78)

A Catholic church dedicated to St Mary was built in the oldest part of Middlesbrough in 1848 to designs by Weightman and Hadfield. This was demolished and replaced by a larger church in 1876–78. Early the following year, it became the cathedral of the newly created See of Middlesbrough. The design, by the nationally renowned Catholic architects George Goldie (1828–87) and Charles Edwin Child (1843–1911) of Kensington, consisted of a nave with aisles, transepts and chancel, plus a lofty tower. The proposed transepts were not built during the first phase of construction but were completed by Edward Goldie (1856–1921) in the 1890s. The proposed 54-foot tower and spire were never built.

Goldie and Child were among the generation of Catholic architects who followed Pugin in his crusade to resurrect the religious architecture and spiritual values of the Middle Ages. Like Pugin, they were trained in a Gothic Revival tradition and were able to design in a medieval spirit. Their scheme for St Mary's emulated the Gothic architecture of the late thirteenth century, while also reflecting the High Victorian taste for polychrome façades.

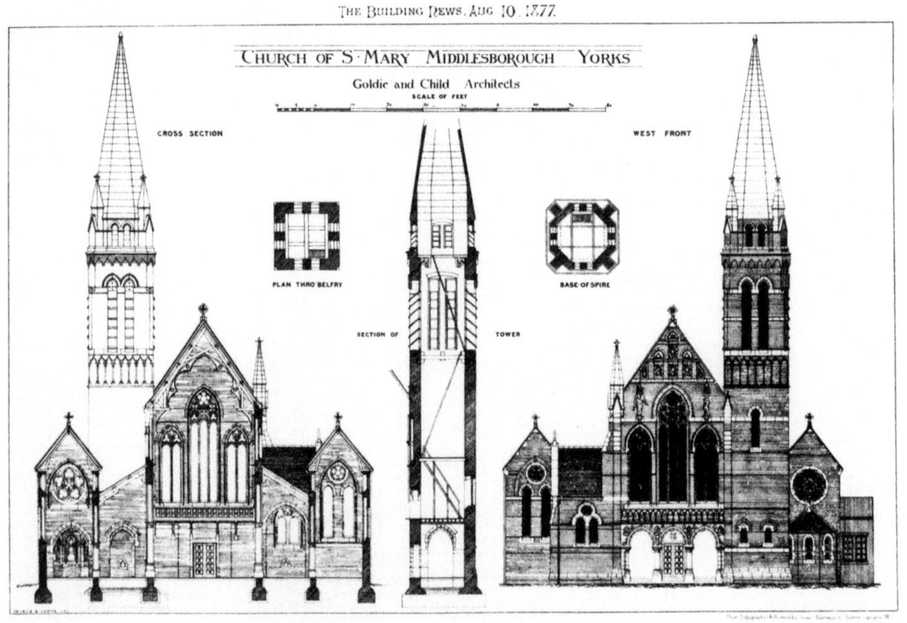

Designs for St Mary's Cathedral published in *Building News* in 1877. (Middlesbrough Libraries and Information)

The great west gable was pierced by windows with Geometrical-style tracery of the early fourteenth century. Below these was a deeply recessed doorway executed in ornamental brickwork and terracotta. Enriching the whole composition were niches containing angelic statues and figures of Our Lady and St Joseph, all of which were sculpted by Thomas Earp (1828–93) of London. Unusually, transepts were built at the extreme west end, giving the church a dominant presence on the street.

Internally, the nave was divided by arches of great lightness and elegance, the space illuminated by a splendid rose window and clerestory. Above the altar was a painting by the sixteenth-century Italian artist Girolamo Cottignola, representing Our Lady and the Divine Infant seated in clouds (1528). The picture had been donated by Henry Bolckow in 1874. The side altars were adorned with pictures presented by John Peter Hornung (1861–1940), a locally born entrepreneur who made a fortune from sugar plantations in East Africa. The north-western altar was surmounted by a painting of Our Lord by N. H. J. Westlake (1833–1921), with saints in adoration. The tide of social change prompted the building of a modern cathedral at Coulby Newham in 1976, as many people began to settle in new housing developments. St Mary's became redundant in the 1990s and eventually burned down in May 2000.

High School, Borough Road (1873–77)

Middlesbrough is fortunate to possess this substantial building by the great Victorian architect Alfred Waterhouse, whose celebrated design for Manchester Town Hall later provided the inspiration for Middlesbrough's own municipal palace. Waterhouse's only confirmed building in Middlesbrough is the former High School, which opened on Borough Road in 1877.

Britain's industrial elite provided innumerable public resources through philanthropy, but in many cases this generosity was calculated to serve their own interests. Employers recognised the value of providing educational resources

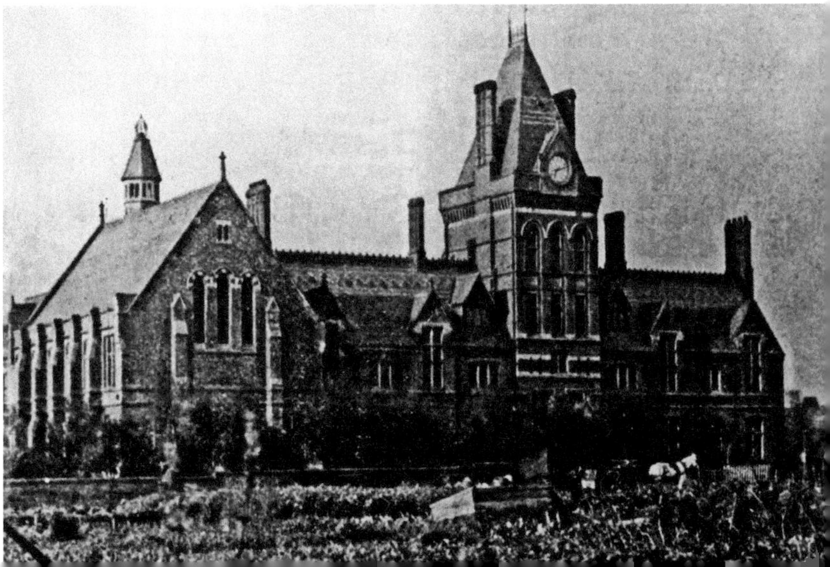

Middlesbrough High School (1873–77), before the demolition of the eastern wing. (Middlesbrough Libraries and Information)

for their employees, ensuring a supply of competent workers. Middlesbrough industrialists met in 1870 to discuss the foundation of a middle-class school to prepare pupils for the Cambridge Local Examinations. Among those present were Henry Bolckow, Thomas Hugh Bell (1844–1931) and Edgar Gilkes (1821–94).

The appointment of Alfred Waterhouse came about through Sir Joseph Whitwell Pease (1828–1903) of Darlington, who was an important client of Waterhouse, as well as a friend and fellow Quaker. Pease had first engaged the young architect to design a modest reading room and teacher's house in the Quaker-dominated resort of Allonby. He influenced the decision to ask Waterhouse to design the Town Hall, rather than initiate a competition. When this came to nothing, it was Pease who gained Waterhouse the commission to design the school and offered a site at the southern end of Albert Road for its construction.

Waterhouse designed an institutional red-brick building with a broad façade and an imposing central tower. Stolid in form, the tower ends with a French pavilion roof, twisting brick chimneys and a mosaic clock face made by Gillett & Bland of Croydon. The use of the Gothic style, with its historical connotations, defined the building as a prestigious middle-class school, in contrast to the Queen Anne-style Board Schools introduced by the Elementary Education Act of 1870. A product of Victorian paternalism, the High School displayed the arms of J. W. Pease and Middlesbrough Corporation. The gable also bears the formidable motto *Aut disce aut discede* ('Either learn or leave').

The school was built by J. Johnson of Auckland at a cost of £10,295. The architectural carving was executed by Farmer & Brindley, who collaborated with Waterhouse on over 100 buildings, including the archetypal Manchester Town Hall and the Natural History Museum in London. The interior featured mosaic flooring by the renowned firm of Jesse Rust & Co. of Battersea and decorative tiles by William Godwin, whose work was based on medieval prototypes. Still visible are Waterhouse's foliated cornices and a roundel based on the Ancient Greek acanthus motif.

Waterhouse's association with the school continued with the design of several extensions, including an east wing for technical education (1884–85) at a cost of £3,820, chemical laboratories (1885–86) at £1,385 and an additional wing (1888–90) at £2,575. These later wings featured tiles by Craven Dunnill, the firm that produced the lavish tilework for Manchester Town Hall. In the 1960s, the building was purchased by Constantine Technical College, which later became Teesside University. Sadly, the school's entire eastern wing was demolished in 1967.

Railway Station, Zetland Road (1874–77)

The Stockton and Darlington Railway was extended to Middlesbrough in 1830, connecting with the new coal port on the Tees. Middlesbrough's first passenger station was built in 1847 to designs by John Middleton.

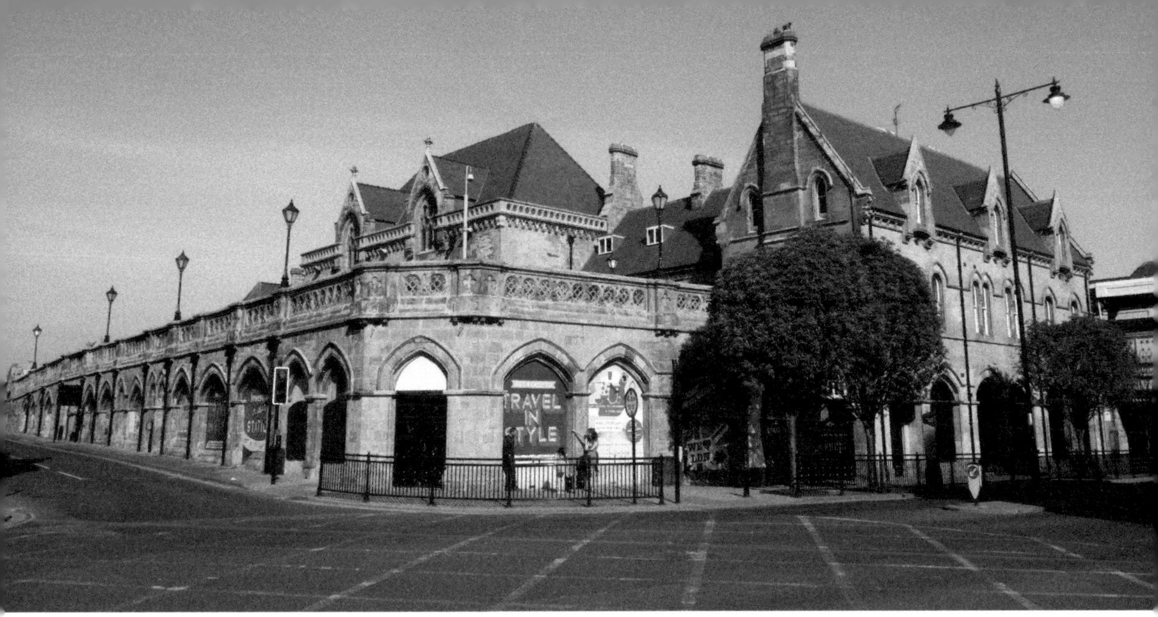

Middlesbrough's neo–Gothic railway station (1874–77).

Unable to cope with the increased traffic of the expanding town, however, the building was demolished in 1874 and replaced by the current station, which opened three years later.

The Stockton and Darlington Railway had merged with the North Eastern Railway in 1863 but retained a distinct identity as the 'Darlington Section'. Its directors clearly took pride in Middlesbrough's success, as they rewarded the town with a prestigious building by their chief architect William Peachey (1826–1912). This was designed in collaboration with William Cudworth, engineer for the Darlington Section, who devised the basic layout of platforms and tracks. Middlesbrough Station was the first in the North East to embrace the Gothic Revival, echoing the neo-medieval design of St Pancras Station in London. Its dominant feature was a train shed of unparalleled verticality.

Because the railway passed over Albert Road, the entire station had to be built upon a vast carriage ramp, lifting it above street level. This created a sprawling forecourt, with shops housed under the supporting arches. In designing the station, Peachey was careful to give each part a distinct identity. The bold mass of the booking hall is dominant on Zetland Road, although the iron porte cochère that once sheltered passengers as they alighted from carriages has been removed. The lofty booking hall was the first of three increasingly large spaces. Next was the concourse, originally covered by a vaulted roof. Passing through a cast-iron arcade, patrons then entered the soaring train shed. Like the gargantuan arch of St Pancras Station, the roof was constructed of wrought-iron lattice girders, but it had a much more vertical aspect, emphasised by a gabled ridge ventilator. The ironwork was supplied by the Derby firm of Andrew Handyside.

The arches rested on masonry piers, but since these were not tied to stop them separating, they relied on the abutment provided by the adjoining buildings and on the vertical thrust of the arches. This had fatal consequences on August Bank

Holiday 1942, when the roof was severely damaged in a German air raid. The remnants were eventually removed in 1954 and replaced by the present concrete roofs, designed by consulting engineer John Dossor.

The entire complex was built at a cost of £100,000. The bulk was executed in Blaxter stone from Northumberland, with roofs of Lakeland and Welsh slate. Contrasting with the medieval power of the stonework are iron and glass platform canopies and bridges more indicative of the industrial age. A subway gave direct communication between the two platforms. Platform 2 boasts an impressive ceramic map of the North Eastern Railway network, made by Craven Dunnill (*c.* 1900).

Middlesbrough Workhouse, New Cemetery Road (1877–78)

Workhouses originated in the Tudor period, but the enduring image of these feared institutions is dominated by the grim buildings of the nineteenth century. Victorian workhouses were introduced by the Poor Law Amendment Act of 1834, which divided England and Wales into Poor Law Unions, each charged with building its own workhouse to accommodate the destitute and homeless. The rationale behind these institutions was not so much to care for the poor, but to punish them for their supposed idleness and to make them pay for their keep by hard labour. As a result, the buildings were designed to intimidate. The Poor Law Commissioners published model workhouse plans and several architects specialised in this building type.

Middlesbrough Poor Law Union was formed in 1875. A 15-acre site in New Cemetery Road (now St Barnabas' Road) was bought at a cost of £6,975 and an architectural competition was held to obtain designs for a workhouse. Twenty-four sets of plans were submitted and Thomas Roger Smith, a London-based architect and surveyor, was appointed to assist the Board of Guardians in their selection. The commission was awarded to William Perkin & Son of Leeds, who had recently completed a workhouse in Chester (1874). However, Smith noted that 'the Local Government Board might require some alteration in the selected plans before they were approved'. Government officials favoured a system of separate pavilions, which facilitated the segregation of inmates and the isolation of infectious diseases. However, the Middlesbrough Guardians feared that this would create an inconvenient building that would be 'cold if only partially occupied' and advocated a corridor plan instead. Ultimately, Perkin modified his design, employing a combination of corridor and pavilion plans.

As built, the workhouse comprised three separate blocks, each catering for different functions. The main building, at the southern end of the site, housed the master's quarters and office, a committee room, clerk's office, strongroom, visitors' room and a large dining room for inmates. Through their layout, workhouse buildings segregated inmates according to age, gender and ability to work. Two symmetrical wings housed male and female 'imbeciles' separately.

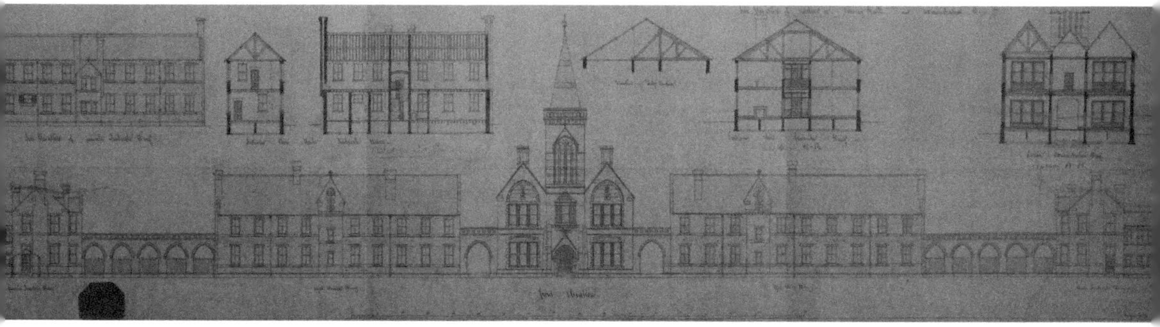

Architects' plans for Middlesbrough Workhouse (1877–78). (Teesside Archives)

An infirmary was situated 60 feet behind the main building, intended for medical cases 'exclusive of fever and infectious diseases'. It comprised a central administration block linked by corridors to the men's and women's pavilions. Segregated schools lay at the north end of the site.

Architecturally, the building had to convey Middlesbrough's civic pride and social conscience, while deterring all but the most destitute from applying for entry. The result was a utilitarian Gothic building in severe red brick with stone dressings. An imposing clock tower was erected over the master's house, rising between the twin gables. Built at a cost of £40,000, the complex was able to accommodate 726 inmates.

After 1930, the main building became a Public Assistance Institution known as the Holgate Institute, while the hospital and school blocks were incorporated into the Municipal Hospital, later the General Hospital. The Holgate Institute became an old people's home in 1948 and was used as an adult training centre from 1974. Most of the main building was demolished in the 1980s. The only material remnant of the workhouse is the Holgate Wall, part of the original perimeter wall, which later enclosed the Holgate end of Ayresome Park football stadium.

Exchange House, Exchange Square (1878–79)

Exchange House was built as a post office by Her Majesty's Office of Works, the official body responsible for the erection of government buildings. The architect was James Williams (1824–92), who designed post offices throughout the country. The building was designed in the baroque style, which carried nationalist connotations due to its association with Wren, Hawksmoor and Vanbrugh, making it suitable for government buildings.

The design is very similar to the Court House that Williams had recently designed for Sunderland (1875). Both buildings feature a ground floor of rusticated sandstone to convey strength and dignity, twin doors in the outer bays and a façade of red brick. The treatment is appropriately restrained, eschewing the theatricality often associated with the baroque style. The doors are emphasised

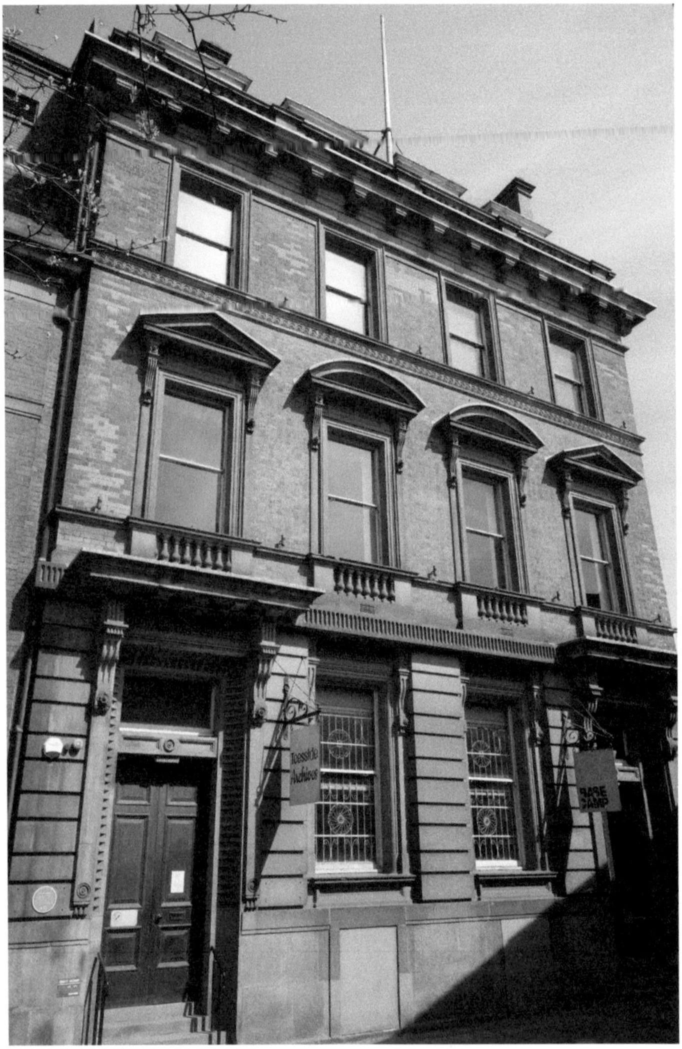

Exchange House (1878–79), overshadowed by the A66 flyover.

by cornices on richly scrolled brackets. Triangular and segmental pediments give variety to the first-floor windows. Details include a Greek key pattern and a guilloche band, consisting of intricate repetitive patterns. The building is surmounted by a prominent cornice, a typically Italian device. In the original Renaissance *palazzi*, the purpose of jutting cornices was to cast a shadow down the façade when the sun was at its highest, but this was scarcely necessary in the northern climate of Middlesbrough.

Exchange House makes a positive contribution to the splendid Victorian streetscape of Exchange Square, but its beauty is severely undermined by the elevated roadway that passes within feet of it. The building serves as the headquarters of Teesside Archives. Following regeneration, part of the property has been transformed into a multifunctional arts space.

St Barnabas's Church, Linthorpe Road (1888–92)

St Barnabas's Church was built for a community that had worshipped in a gymnasium and a cemetery chapel before establishing a permanent home. The first church on this site was built in 1875, but as Linthorpe was developed with fashionable villas, a larger building was proposed. A subscription fund was launched by the Revd John William Dales, who humorously described himself as 'Linthorpe's Champion Beggar'. William Bastiman of Linthorpe was the contractor, who constructed the building at a cost of £3,000. However, the south aisle was not built during the first stage of construction. The original mission church was retained as a church hall until it was replaced by a new structure, designed by Doughty & Sons (1911).

The present church was designed by Charles Hodgson Fowler (1840–1910), one of the leading ecclesiastical architects in the North East. Born in Nottinghamshire, Fowler was trained by the eminent Victorian architect Sir George Gilbert Scott (1811–78) and established independent practice in Durham in 1864. St Barnabas illustrates his ability to create a dignified place of worship on a limited budget. Impressive in its scale, the church comprises a vast nave with aisles, clerestory and a very tall choir. The execution, however, is spartan. Early English Gothic of the late twelfth century is the idiom and plain red brick the predominant material. Even the plate tracery of the great west window is composed of brick rather than stone.

The nave is large enough to accommodate 750 worshippers. The interior is lined with brick and divided by round, octagonal and compound piers. In the

St Barnabas' Church (1888–92), cheaply built but vast in scale.

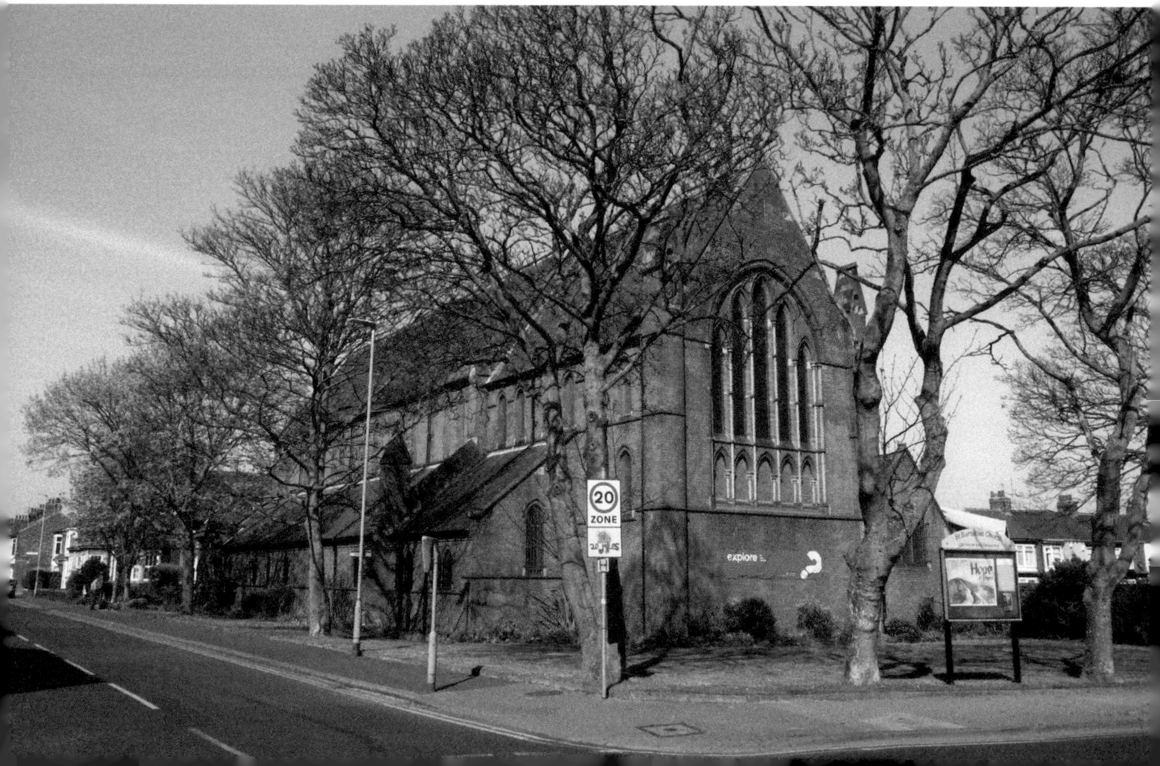

choir are wooden stalls ornamented with poppyheads and traceried panels. A fine chancel screen was carved by R. T. Snaith of Darlington (1928) and features statues of saints within elaborate niches. A musicians' gallery was made by the master woodcarver Robert 'Mouseman' Thompson (1876–1955) of Kilburn in the mid-twentieth century, enhancing this simple, but pious space.

Nos 36–42 Linthorpe Road (1889)

This fine procession of commercial buildings is a prominent feature within the streetscape of Linthorpe Road. Designed by Roger Lofthouse, it takes the form of an elegant terrace with shops on the ground floor and offices above. Like the newspaper offices that Lofthouse designed in Zetland Road, the façade exhibits a Northern Renaissance style that evokes the historic mercantile culture of the Low Countries. The style gave further variety to Middlesbrough's commercial architecture and was eminently more suited to the northern climate than the Italian Renaissance style favoured in the 1870s.

The façade is articulated by two tiers of pilasters, both supporting rich entablatures. Amidst all this fine ornamentation, it is the pilasters that catch the eye. The whole ensemble is enriched with carvings of human figures, mythical beasts, birds, fish and vases of flowers, all of exceptional workmanship. Crowning the building are the elaborately shaped gables characteristic of Dutch and Flemish architecture, between which rise acorn-shaped finials symbolising prosperity.

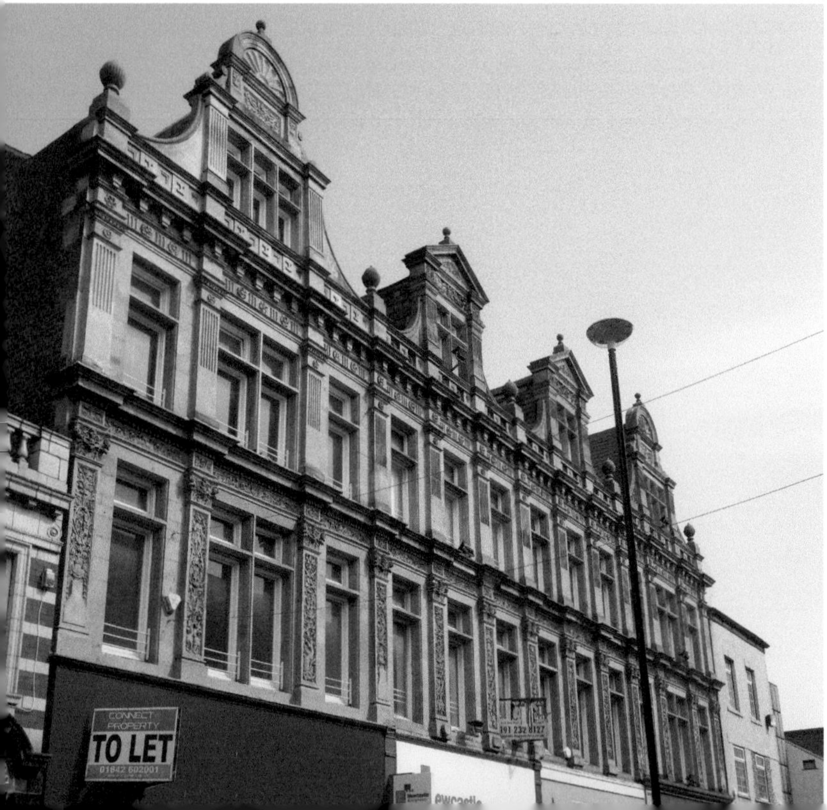

Commercial buildings at Nos 36–42 Linthorpe Road (1889).

Town Hall and Municipal Buildings, Corporation Road (1883–89)

Middlesbrough's original Town Hall was built in 1846 at the centre of the grid-iron streets planned by the town's founding fathers. However, with the town's rapid growth and the shift of its commercial centre, it became imperative to build larger and grander premises south of the railway line. A dignified Town Hall was essential for the prestige of any Victorian metropolis, declaring its importance, prosperity and civic values. Middlesbrough erected a splendid new Town Hall and municipal buildings between Corporation Road and Albert Road in 1883–89. This civic palace became the administrative and ceremonial heart of the Victorian town.

Middlesbrough Corporation considered the best means of obtaining designs for the new building. J. W. Pease recommended awarding the commission directly to Alfred Waterhouse, an architect who had designed several public, commercial and domestic buildings for the industrialist and fellow Quaker. Waterhouse was at that time engaged in work on Manchester Town Hall. The councillors debated whether to award the commission to Waterhouse 'or some other eminent architect', or to hold an open competition, eventually voting four to three in favour of Pease's proposition. Waterhouse produced a design in 1873–75, but this was not executed, perhaps due to the lack of a viable site.

In January 1877, the Corporation purchased 7,466 square yards of land from the Owners of the Middlesbrough Estate for £8,428 5*s*. 0*d*. An open competition was held in April 1882 for the design of a Town Hall containing a council room, committee rooms, offices for the Town Clerk, Borough Surveyor and Borough Accountant, a police court, drill ground, free library and offices for the School Board. Eleven sets of drawings were submitted anonymously, and Waterhouse was elected at a salary of 100 guineas to judge them, probably at the behest of Joseph Pease to make up for the earlier disappointment. His decision was announced on 13 June 1882 and the first prize of £300 was awarded to a plan marked with the pseudonym 'Law and Order'. This was drawn by G. G. Hoskins of Darlington,

G. G. Hoskins' design for Middlesbrough Town Hall and Municipal Buildings, published in *The Builder* (1889).

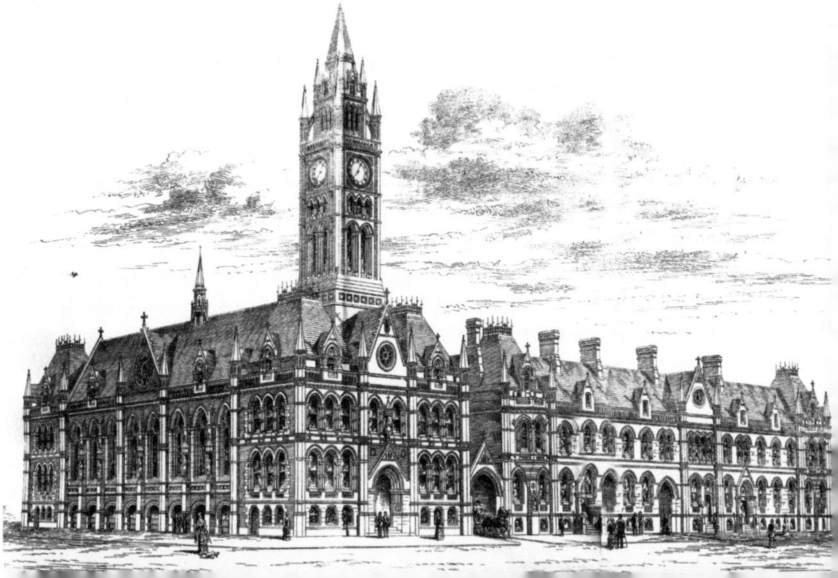

a Gothic specialist who had served as Waterhouse's clerk of works on several local projects. While it is possible that Waterhouse was aware of the design's provenance, he acted as adjudicator in many architectural competitions and was regarded as a highly professional and reliable judge. The contract for construction was awarded to Messrs E. Atkinson.

The architect considered the advisability of using stone or brick for the building's external facing and after inspecting the principal buildings in Middlesbrough, he arrived at the conclusion that:

> Stone buildings suffer too greatly from the effects of the smoke caused by the several industries of the district, and consequently assume a dark and gloomy monotony, whereas buildings of brick, if liberally relieved with stone dressings, present a pleasing contrast, even under the inevitable effects of smoke-stain.

Hoskins decided on a combination of brick and stone and published a design prescribing these materials in *Building News* in January 1883. In execution, however, the building was faced entirely with stone. On 24 October 1883, an octagonal foundation stone was laid at the north-east corner, as part of one of the clasping buttresses.

Majestic in conception, the Town Hall was designed in thirteenth-century French Gothic style and built of hard Yorkshire stone at the astonishing cost of £130,000. Unsurprisingly, Hoskins' design shows the influence of Manchester Town Hall, a masterpiece of civic Gothic architecture. However, the rectangular site was much more convenient than the triangular one at Manchester, enabling Hoskins to give the building a simpler, more regular plan. The complex consists of the Town Hall building on Corporation Road and municipal buildings to the south, arranged around a quadrangle.

The northern façade is stately and symmetrical, with dominant pavilions at the ends, accentuated by octagonal buttresses. As at Manchester, French pavilion

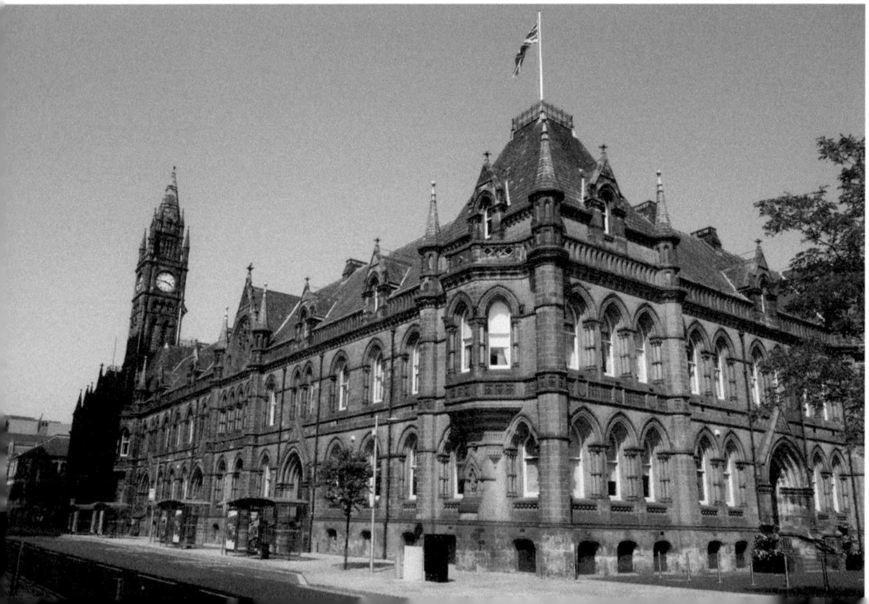

Town Hall and Municipal Buildings (1883–89), majestic in French Gothic style.

roofs with iron balustrades crown the building. Hoskins' original design did not include the present porch. This was a later addition, prompted by one of the worst tragedies of the Victorian era.

In June 1883, the Victoria Hall in Sunderland became the scene of a disaster when 183 children were crushed to death in a rush to get prizes at a children's show. The disaster resulted in new legislation demanding outward-opening exits for all such places of entertainment and Hoskins, who designed the ill-fated building in 1872, was forced to defend himself in the building press. Fears of a recurrence prompted the building of an additional exit at Middlesbrough. With insufficient space to erect an outward-facing porch, Hoskins arranged the steps laterally along the façade, leading to doors at the sides of the porch, rather than on the frontage. Unfortunately, the addition of the porch obscured the lower half of the two central windows and produced an awkward effect.

The main entrance lies at the centre of the Albert Road elevation, which resembles the east face of Manchester Town Hall. Above the door is a shield emblazoned with Middlesbrough's coat of arms and its motto, *Erimus*. An immense clock tower rises above the entrance, dominating views along Corporation Road and Albert Road. Built at a cost of £882, the tower is 170 feet tall, surmounted by a spire, pinnacles and gablets.

The municipal buildings are divided from the Town Hall by a longitudinal carriage driveway, which opens onto Albert Road and Dunning Street. Both entrances are framed by elaborate Gothic arches, one of which retains its original iron gate. The passage was roofed using Rendle's patent system of glazing. The municipal buildings follow a quadrangular plan, ultimately derived from medieval monasteries, which allowed the offices to be lit with natural light via the courtyard. As in the main building, the corners are treated as pavilions and the central bay of each face is crested by a gable and rose window. Oriel windows project from the pavilions on Albert Road and the central bay overlooking Victoria Square.

Allegorical sculptures served the dual purpose of articulating the function of each individual block and proclaiming the civic values that the building was intended to embody. Figures of St George and the Dragon stand over the entrance on Albert Road, proclaiming Middlesbrough's nationalist loyalties, while Justice is represented above the entrance to the former police court in Dunning Street. The frontage along Corporation Road is arrayed with statues representing Music, Painting, Literature and Commerce, each standing within a canopied niche. A fifth figure, representing Science, had to be omitted due to the addition of the aforementioned porch. Together, the statues portrayed Middlesbrough as a cultural and intellectual centre, as well as an industrial powerhouse. The statues were sculpted by William Margetson of Chelsea, chiselled from Yorkshire stone at a cost of £50 each.

The interior boasts a stately Council Chamber with oak panelling around the walls, decorated with trefoils, and a heavy stone fireplace. Stalls for borough officials were provided along one wall and at the centre stood a grand chair for

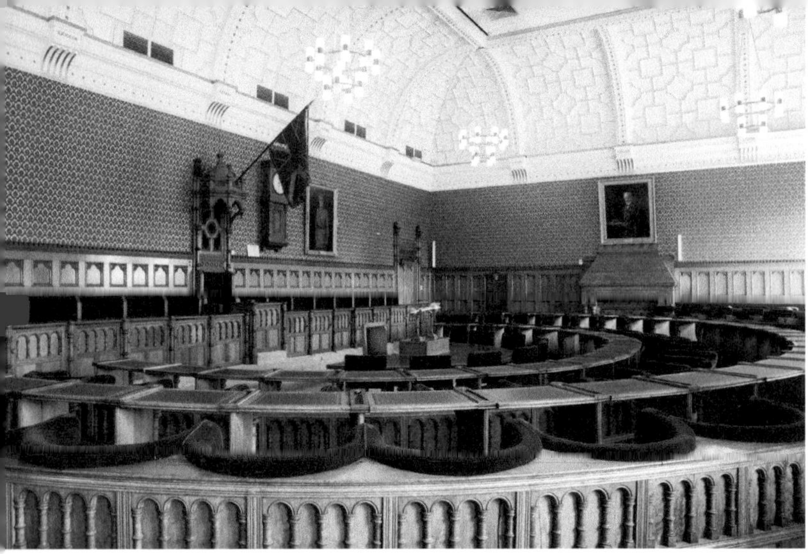

The lavish Council Chamber. (Middlesbrough Council)

the mayor, beneath a Gothic canopy. Still surviving is the Magistrates' Court, which was hailed as 'the finest court of its description in the country'. The space is lit by a skylight set into an elaborate lantern ceiling. The suspended glass panels display the scales and sword of justice and the symbols of England, Scotland and Ireland, a rose, thistle and shamrock, respectively. Stairs lead to the twelve police cells below.

The largest and most impressive interior is the grand Concert Hall, which features a double hammer-beam roof made of local steel. Fixed to each beam is a dragon gargoyle holding a gas pipe in its mouth. When in use, this system of gas lighting would have given the fantastical impression that the hall was illuminated by dragon fire. The walls originally displayed full-length portraits of Pease, Bolckow, Vaughan and other members of Middlesbrough's industrial pantheon. The floor of the hall was built using 'Dennett's fire-proof construction', a system that Hoskins had previously used at the Backhouse Bank in Albert Road. As well as protecting against fire, this system of concrete arches supported by iron ribs obviated the need for columns in the police drill hall immediately below, which would have interfered with manoeuvres.

As Middlesbrough continued to develop in the twentieth century, many of the civic functions of the Town Hall required purpose-built premises. The library transferred to the new Central Library in 1912 and new police headquarters opened in Dunning Street in 1962. A modern civic centre was constructed alongside the Victorian building in 1971–73, connected to its predecessor by Middlesbrough's own Bridge of Sighs. Designed by Borough Architect J. V. Wall, this brutalist building is notable for its concrete exoskeleton surrounding walls of engineering brick. In 2016, the Town Hall closed for a £7.7m refurbishment funded by Middlesbrough Council and the Heritage Lottery Fund.

Middlesbrough Town Hall was one of the last Gothic town halls in Britain. Replacing the modest building that had served the embryonic town, it exemplified the civic pride and prosperity of the late Victorian era, when Middlesbrough, the 'infant Hercules', reached maturity.

Bell Brothers Offices, Zetland Road (1881–91)

This architectural gem, dating from the late Victorian period, is the finest building in Middlesbrough. Built as offices for Bell Brothers, the renowned ironmasters, it is the only surviving commercial building designed by Philip Webb, a pioneer of the Arts and Crafts movement. Completed in 1891, it was the culmination of an unlikely, but highly productive relationship between the Bell family and the father of Arts and Crafts architecture.

Sir Isaac Lowthian Bell (1816–1904) and his two brothers founded a company in 1844 to lease a furnace at Wylam. In 1854, they established the Clarence Works on the north bank of the Tees, building three blast furnaces. Major salt deposits were discovered at the Clarence Works in 1863, enabling the firm to establish a chemical plant that laid the foundation for the Teesside chemical industry.

Philip Webb began his career as an articled pupil of the renowned Gothic architect G. E. Street, who designed Middlesbrough's All Saints' Church. In Street's office, Webb became friends with William Morris, whose work, philosophy and Socialist politics were the basis for the Arts and Crafts movement. Morris and his followers were appalled by the effects of the Industrial Revolution, particularly the labour conditions inherent in the factory system. Many shared Marx's view that industrial capitalism was inherently exploitative, condemning workers to

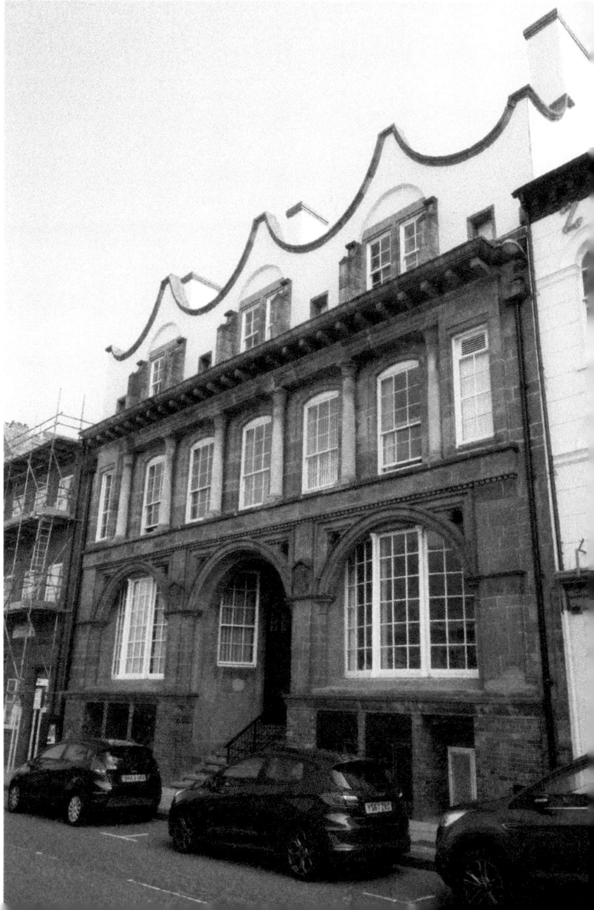

Bell Brothers' offices (1881–91), Philip Webb's only surviving commercial building.

alienating labour in a mechanised system of mass production. As an antidote to industrialisation, they aimed to revive the craft traditions of pre-industrial England and developed principles of good design that allowed workers to take pride in their craft.

Webb designed Morris's matrimonial home, the Red House at Bexleyheath in Kent (1859), which became the cornerstone of Arts and Crafts architecture. Believing that buildings must relate to their surroundings, Webb drew inspiration from vernacular traditions. He also advocated mastery of building craft through direct contact with materials and insisted on the finest craftmanship in his buildings.

Despite their Socialist principles, Arts and Crafts designers were often dependent upon the patronage of the Victorian bourgeoisie, since it was mainly affluent clients who could afford the products of their idealistic craft system. In 1864, Webb accepted a commission to enlarge Bell's house, Washington Hall in County Durham. Bell moved in Pre-Raphaelite circles and it may have been John Ruskin who suggested Webb's appointment. A friendship developed between architect and client, which lasted until Bell's death in 1904. Working for Bell's son, Hugh, Webb designed Red Barns, at Coatham near Redcar in 1868–70. This was followed by one of Webb's finest country houses, Rounton Grange near Northallerton, which he designed for the Bell family (1872–76). Sadly, the house was demolished in 1953.

Domestic projects were Webb's métier, but his friendship with the Bell family brought him a number of industrial commissions that tested his principles. In 1867, Lowthian Bell asked him to design a clock tower for the Clarence Works, stating that, 'We have no wish to make the affair an expensive one, but I wish to avoid making it ridiculous.' Like other Arts and Crafts practitioners, Webb abhorred industry, but out of loyalty to his friend he accepted the commission. Strict timing was required in the smelting of iron, so the tower had two clocks, each facing a bank of furnaces, and a third facing the river. Webb designed a dignified structure, with bells on the upper stage, perhaps in reference to the client's name.

In 1873, Webb was asked to design an aesthetic treatment for a new blowing engine house, the dimensions of the building having already been determined by the firm's draughtsman. Webb must have hated working in this manner, which contravened his design philosophy. However, he devised a monumental brick structure with tall Romanesque arches rising from the foundations and smaller, corbelled arches to support water tanks on the roof. This was followed by new offices for the Clarence Works. Again, Webb relied on brick detailing and powerful arches, probably as a tribute to the great Roman engineers. The four corner 'pyramids', as Webb termed the pavilions, may have been a deliberate reference to those at Rounton Grange. Sadly, all of Webb's buildings at the Clarence Works were demolished in the 1970s.

The climax of Webb's work for the Bell family is the superb office building at Middlesbrough. In 1881, Hugh Bell asked him to design larger premises for the firm on the site of their existing offices near the railway station. Webb's earliest surviving drawings date from 1883, but a severe downturn in trade delayed construction. The scheme was revived in August 1889 and John Johnson of

Middlesbrough was contracted to build the offices at a cost of £6,440. The stone came from Scarth Nick Quarry in the Yorkshire Dales, and the masons were taken to Rounton Grange to see the precise finish that Webb demanded.

In contrast to the buildings erected by rival firms, the Bell Brothers offices are exceptionally graceful, relying on inventive detail and superb craftsmanship rather than bombastic effects. Webb's primary concern was to provide good light in all rooms. For this reason, he raised the ground floor above street level and placed the main offices on the first floor, lifting them above the shadow cast by the railway buildings opposite. A central door was provided 'for instant communications and best light', leading to a lightwell at the core of the building. The basement is lined with glazed brown bricks and lit by windows with wrought iron grills.

In composing the façade, Webb initially envisioned two-storey bow windows. However, he must have decided that this would look weak, as the final building has bow windows on the ground floor only, recessed behind powerful arches. This solution was based on an abortive scheme he had prepared for commercial buildings in Newcastle (1866). It is likely that Webb was recommended for this project by Lowthian Bell, who was the Vice-Chairman of Newcastle Corporation's Finance Committee. Aware that large shop windows on the ground floor can create a visual weakness, Webb used huge round arches to counteract the large areas of glass. At Middlesbrough, the arches spring from slender hexagonal pilasters with trumpet-shaped capitals.

The first floor follows a different rhythm, with segmental windows interposed between columns with waterleaf capitals. An exaggerated cornice terminates this storey and three attic dormers echo the three divisions of the ground floor, thereby unifying the façade. Sweeping concave gables form a distinctive roofline, creating a wave-like effect. The gables were intended to be of exposed brick, but Webb realised that brick would be blackened by industrial smoke, so he covered them in render, which could be repainted periodically.

The upper walls were supported by great 'bressumer beams', functioning like lintels. All the latest building technologies and conveniences were incorporated, although a proposed passenger lift was never installed. Much like his architect, Hugh Bell took a personal interest in every detail of the building. A private rear entrance and spiral stair led to his first-floor office. There was also a system whereby he received a four-minute warning when his train was due at the station.

Webb's successor George Jack made alterations to the offices in 1906, including the addition of two large rooms on the attic floor and the insertion of extra steel beams to carry the additional weight. Dorman, Long and Co. took over Bell Brothers in 1902 and acquired the building when they liquidated all their subsidiary companies in 1923. The building narrowly escaped demolition when new urban roadways were ploughed into the heart of Middlesbrough in the 1980s. It has now been converted to flats and workshops. One of only two commercial buildings ever designed by Philip Webb, and the only one to survive, it is the most architecturally significant building in Middlesbrough. The ingenious design is remarkably daring in its choice of motifs and the freedom of their handling.

Hugh Bell School, Grange Road (1892)

The impressive Grange Road Schools stood at the edge of Victoria Square, forming a superb architectural ensemble with the Town Hall and the Central Library. In 1898, the schools were renamed in honour of the chemical manufacturer Sir Hugh Bell, who was mayor of Middlesbrough for three terms. Bell was the son of the pioneering ironmaster Sir Isaac Lowthian Bell and the father of adventurer Gertrude Bell.

The schools were designed in the Queen Anne style synonymous with the urban Board Schools that were built after the Education Act of 1870. While the publicly funded Board Schools were often constrained by budgetary limitations, however, the Grange Road School was a product of private philanthropy, a fact reflected in its lavish design.

Occupying a generous site, the building had only two main storeys, making it less intimidating than the towering Board Schools. The decorous façades were encrusted with terracotta ornament, a material that was both economical and resistant to atmospheric pollution, a valuable attribute in a hive of industry such as Middlesbrough. A parade of Dutch gables gave the building a distinctive skyline, enhanced by a wonderfully delicate tower overlooking Borough Road.

Hugh Bell School (1892). (Middlesbrough Libraries and Information)

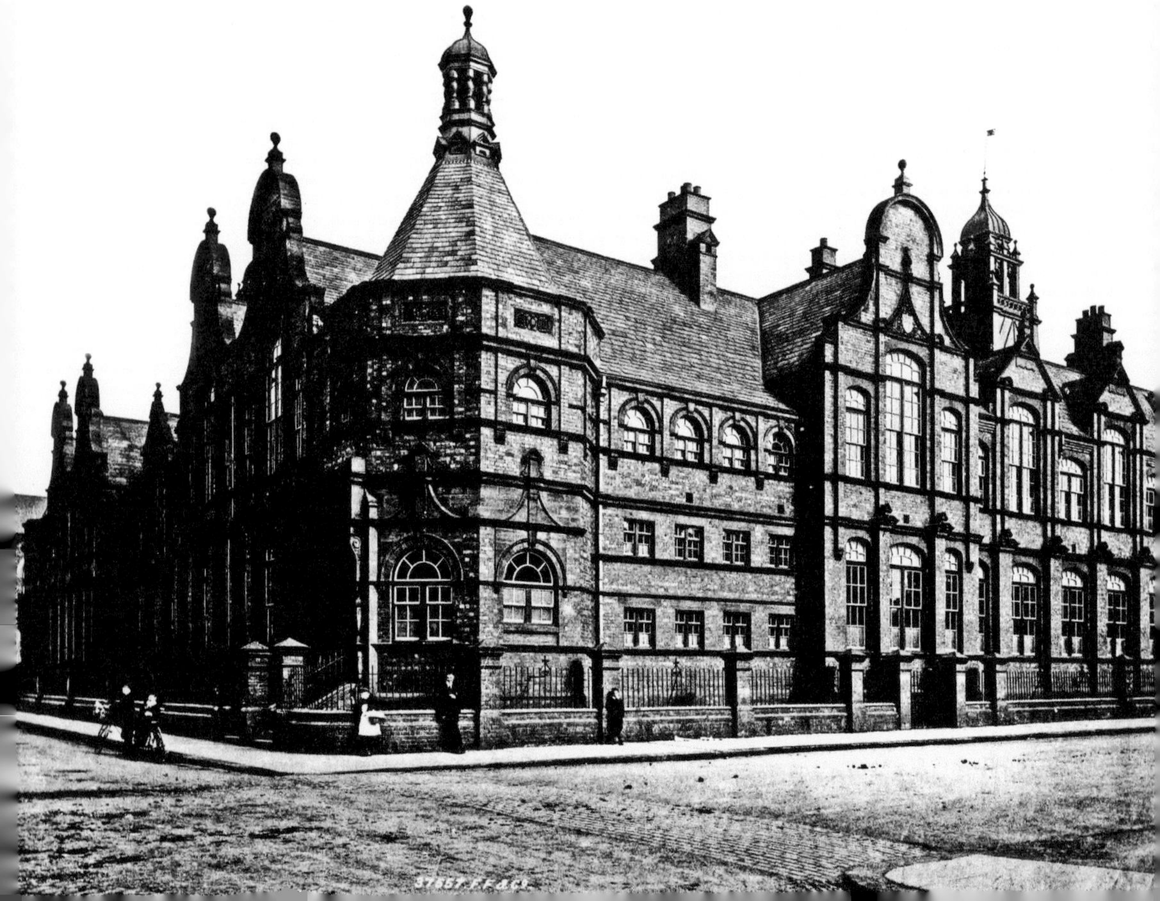

Despite its merits, the building was demolished in 1969 to make way for the modernist slab of Teesside Magistrates' Court (1970–73), designed by Borough Architect J. V. Wall and his staff.

Empire Palace of Varieties, Corporation Road (1897–99)

The Empire Palace of Varieties was a spectacular place of entertainment built at the end of the nineteenth century. The theatre was built by William Bastiman and designed by Ernest Runtz (1859–1913) of London, who had a successful commercial and theatre practice until a series of financial problems bankrupted him in 1912. He worked mainly in a baroque style, often displaying Continental influences.

Standing on Corporation Road, the theatre was designed to group well with the adjacent Town Hall. Stylistically, the building is unique, exuding a spectacular Spanish Renaissance style never before seen in Britain. The façade is a secular rendition of Spanish cathedrals such as Jaén, with twin towers at the extremities and an arcaded façade between them. Utilising the latest building technologies, the theatre was built on a steel frame provided by Dorman Long, together with walls of Normanby brick. The entire structure was clad in terracotta by the renowned firm of Doulton & Co. of Lambeth. The vivid ornamentation includes griffins, cartouches and floral garlands. Cut into the façade is an arcaded mezzanine and the arches are divided by fantastical colonnettes with tulip-shaped bases and flame finials. Reflecting avant-garde trends of the *fin de siècle*, there is a row of female faces in art nouveau style.

Inside, the foyer features Roman Doric columns in marble and a frieze decorated with rinceaux, or swirling foliage forms. The auditorium is horseshoe shaped, with two tiers of seating, as well as six private boxes, supported on giant

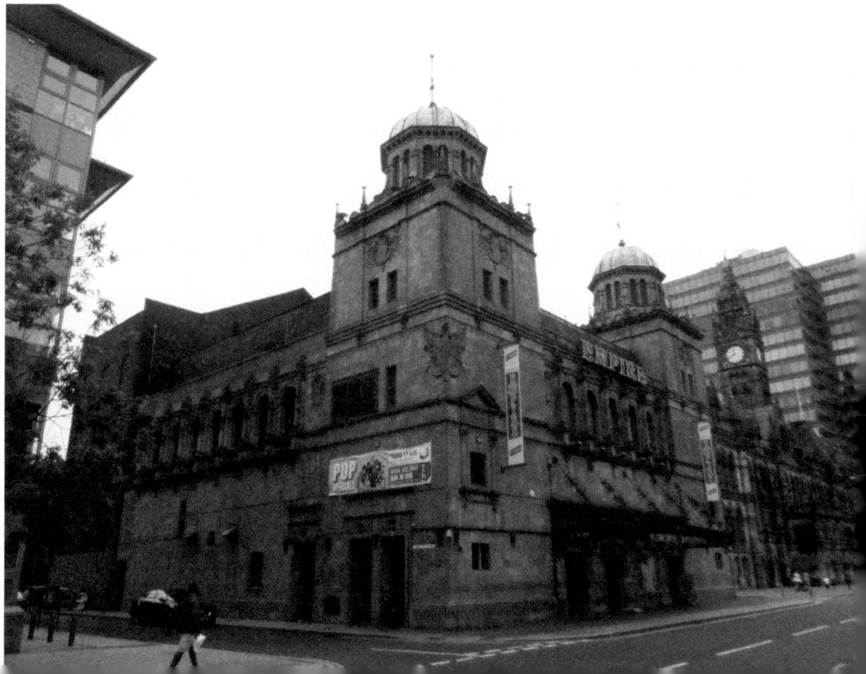

Empire Palace of Varieties (1897–99), in Spanish Renaissance style.

scrolled brackets. Middlesbrough once boasted many theatres and music halls, but the Empire is the only one still standing. Having hosted stars such as Charlie Chaplin and Houdini, it spent a period as a bingo hall and is now a nightclub and events venue.

Forbes' Buildings, Linthorpe Road (1899–1900)

Forbes' Buildings were erected as commercial premises for John Forbes in 1899–1900. Arriving from Aberdeen in 1875, Forbes established a bakery in Lower Feversham Street. He was later able to erect these purpose-built premises on Linthorpe Road, consisting of a bakery, shops and offices, with stables at the rear. A prosperous businessman and public figure, Forbes was elected mayor of Middlesbrough in 1904.

This highly exuberant building was designed by Roger Lofthouse & Sons of Middlesbrough, who provided an inventive design with a range of charming details. The practice consisted of Lofthouse and his sons James Alfred Earnest (d. 1929) and Thomas Aston (d. 1914). By the turn of the century, the baroque style was being used in a very free manner and, together with the emergence of art nouveau, this encouraged fluid architectural forms. Forbes' Buildings is a product of this increasingly abstract approach.

The broad façade is broken into an arrhythmic series of gables, creating a varied roofline. The tallest gables are pierced by Venetian windows, consisting of an arched central light flanked by sidelights. The playful effect is enhanced by the use of red brick and dressings of buff terracotta, producing a vibrant colour scheme. Both the style and materials were widely used in commercial architecture at the

The sprawling Forbes' Buildings (1899–1900), in art nouveau style.

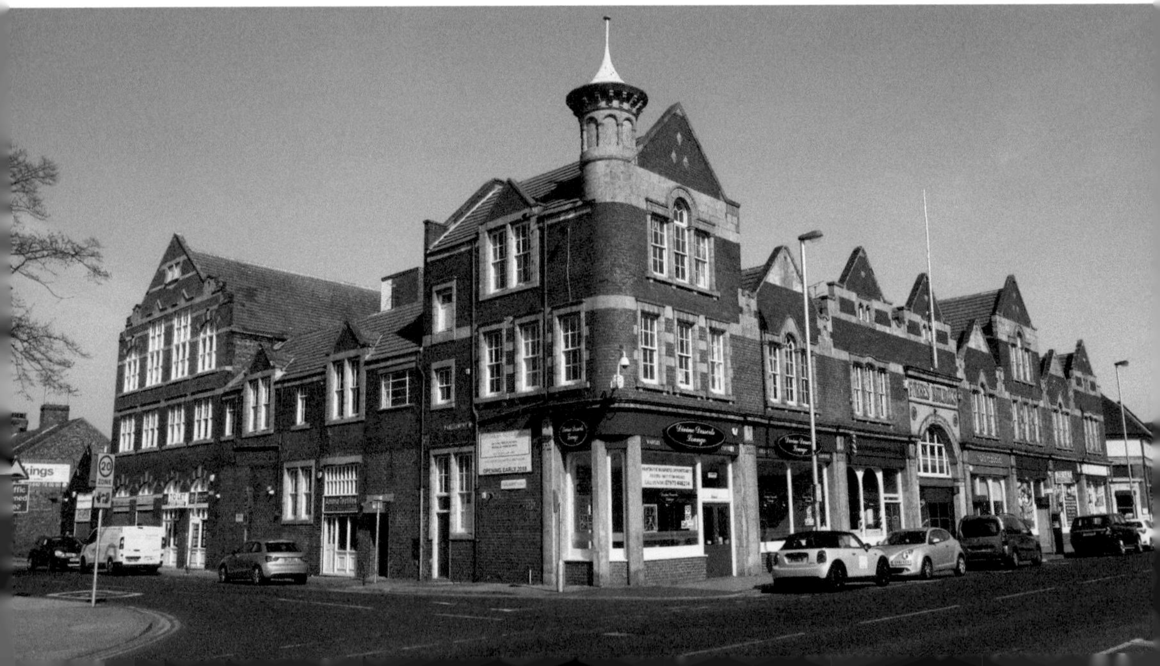

turn of the century. Focal points of the design are the graceful turret that turns the corner from Linthorpe Road to Parliament Road and the ornate archway that punctuates the frontage. Above this grand entrance, the building's name is executed in art nouveau lettering. The building is now used as a shopping arcade.

St Cuthbert's Church, Newport Road (1897–1901)

St Cuthbert's Church was built to take 5,000 worshipers from the overburdened parish of St Paul. The driving force behind its construction was Thomas Enraght Lindsay, minister at St Paul's, whose parishioners numbered an incredible 30,000. Built by Allison Brothers of Middlesbrough, the huge edifice was designed to accommodate a congregation of 825.

The church is an important work by Temple Lushington Moore, one of the most imaginative architects of the late Gothic Revival. Born at Tullamore in Ireland, Moore was raised in Glasgow, where his father served as Staff Officer of Pensioners in the British Army. In 1872, Moore left Glasgow to study in the East Riding of Yorkshire. Here he developed a deep love of the county and settled upon a career in architecture. The greatest concentration of his work was in the East Riding. Working during the last phase of the Gothic Revival, Moore did not simply prolong a dying tradition, but brought it to maturity, completing the majestic history of Gothic architecture as it evolved from the medieval to the modern age. His work reveals a brilliantly imaginative reworking of traditional forms and an aesthetic of extreme simplicity. The critic H. S. Goodhart-Rendel (1887–1959) attributed this austerity to the influence of the great abbeys of Yorkshire and memorably stated that Moore 'spoke Gothic with a Yorkshire accent'. In fact, his influences were considerably more diverse.

St Cuthbert's was a church for an area with a 'great working-class population'. With a modest budget of £10,000, it was built of brick, but faced with stone from Carlton and Swainby, 8 miles to the south. Moore invariably employed local stone in his projects, which saved money and helped to relate each building to its locality.

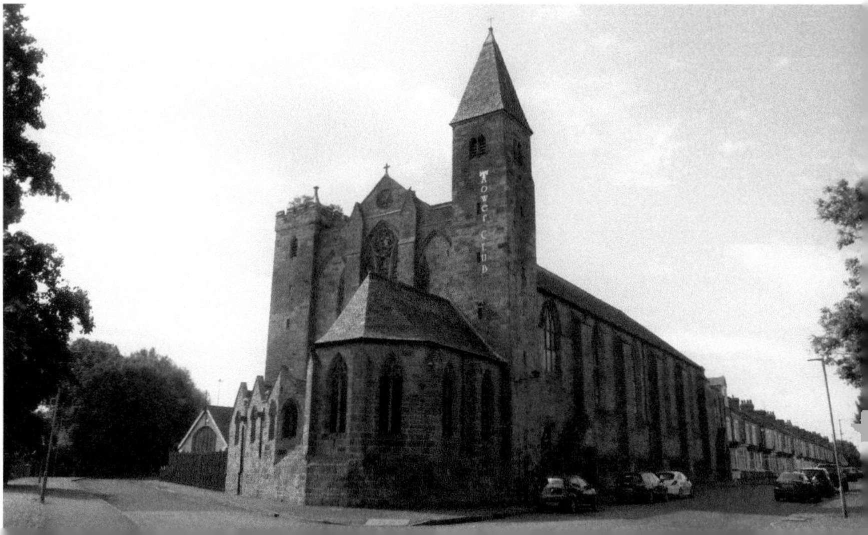

St Cuthbert's Church (1897–1901), designed by Temple Moore.

Reflecting its industrial setting, the church is powerfully austere, rising from a simple rectangular base. However, an octagonal baptistry and gabled vestry are massed at the east end, canted to fit into the sharply angled site. Above these, the east face rises sheer and fortress-like, braced by strong buttresses and slender towers. Moore frequently incorporated such towers into his churches, sometimes as stair turrets or bell towers and sometimes simply for visual effect. They were probably derived from the square stair turrets of Romanesque churches in Normandy. The resulting asymmetrical silhouette is typical of Moore, who frequently used asymmetry to create dramatic contrasts. An early design for St Cuthbert's shows a conventional east window, but in execution Moore split up the lights into a 1-3-1 configuration. He repeated this technique in ten of his subsequent churches, grouping the lights in various permutations. This solution was probably influenced by Continental examples such as Paderborn Cathedral in Germany.

In keeping with the exterior, Moore devised an internal space of great simplicity. The aisles were reduced to narrow passages to create a nave of maximum capacity. This was a solution developed by architects such as G. F. Bodley as they adapted medieval church typologies to the needs of large urban congregations. The passage aisles, cut through square piers of the utmost severity, were immensely tall and slender, giving the interior a vertical emphasis. The oversailing arches of the arcades were unmoulded and unchamfered, a key feature of Moore's vocabulary for town churches. Also typical of Moore were the wooden vaulting of the roof and the arches that pierce the wall behind the altar to reveal the spaces beyond.

The church was decommissioned in 1972 and now operates as a dance school. The interior has been disrupted by the insertion of a new floor and a ceiling that obscures the soaring vault. Despite these alterations and its undeniably bleak surroundings, St Cuthbert's Church survives as a testament to Temple Moore's mastery of modern Gothic architecture.

St Columba's Church, Cannon Street (1900–02)

At a passing glance, St Columba's Church could easily be dismissed as a crudely executed building for a working-class parish, a misshapen hulk in cheap industrial brick. In fact, this is one of the most advanced buildings in Middlesbrough, designed by the last master of the Gothic Revival, Temple Moore, and its unorthodox design is thrillingly inventive.

In 1896, the Archbishop of York, William MacLagan, authorised the building of a new church to serve the working-class community around Cannon Street, which numbered 28,000. A site was purchased in November 1897 for £1,700 and a Million Penny Fund was started in September 1900. The final building belonged to the High Church tradition and was designed to accommodate 600 parishioners.

Standing less than a mile from Moore's slightly earlier church of St Cuthbert, this was indeed a cheap church for a poor district. A large urban church such

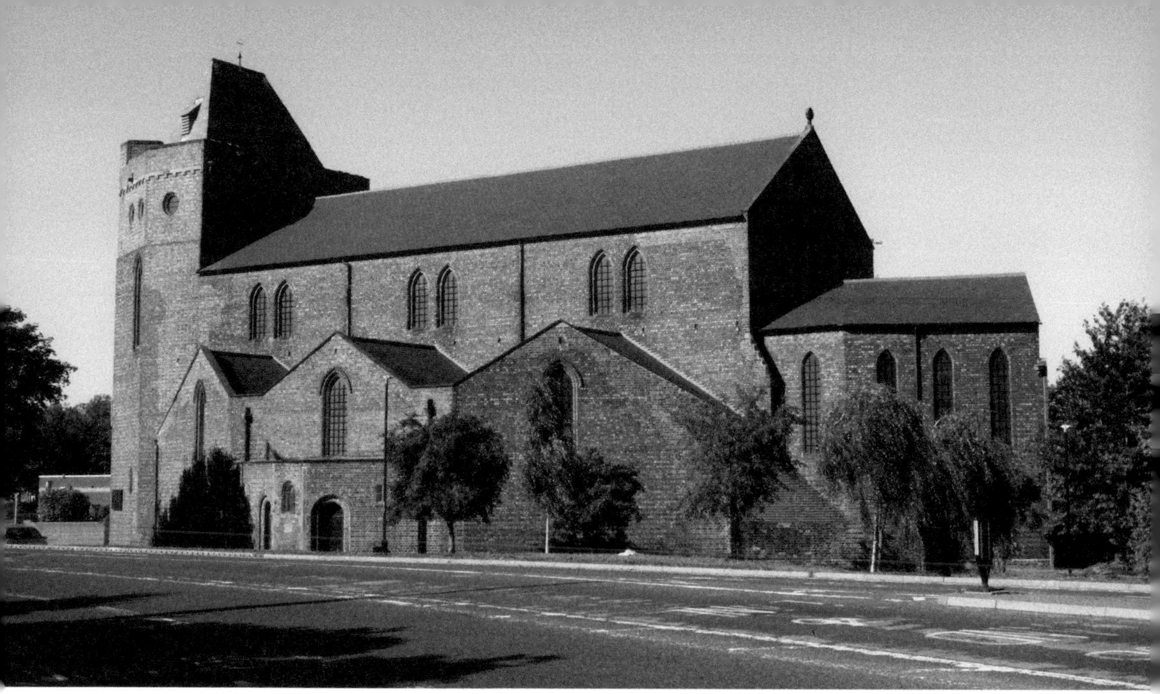

Above: The uncompromising neo–Gothic of St Columba's Church (1900–02).

Right: St Columba's tower, powerfully echoing a German *westwerk*.

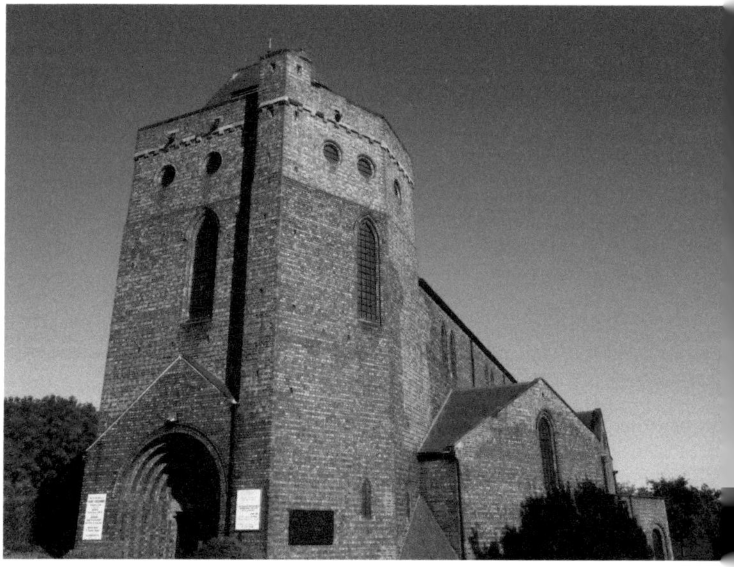

as this represented a difficult brief. The site was highly irregular and, with a budget of only £7,000, the design had to be economical. Moore's initial design of 1898 proposed a conventional rectangular church squeezed onto the rhombic site but leaving much of the space unoccupied. However, he subsequently devised an ingenious scheme to maximise the multi-angled site with a plan resembling a distorted octagon. Through inventive design, Moore managed to achieve the impression of a conventional nave, filling the remainder of the site with aisles canted at their east and west ends. The resulting play of dynamic angles anticipates the German expressionist architecture of the 1920s.

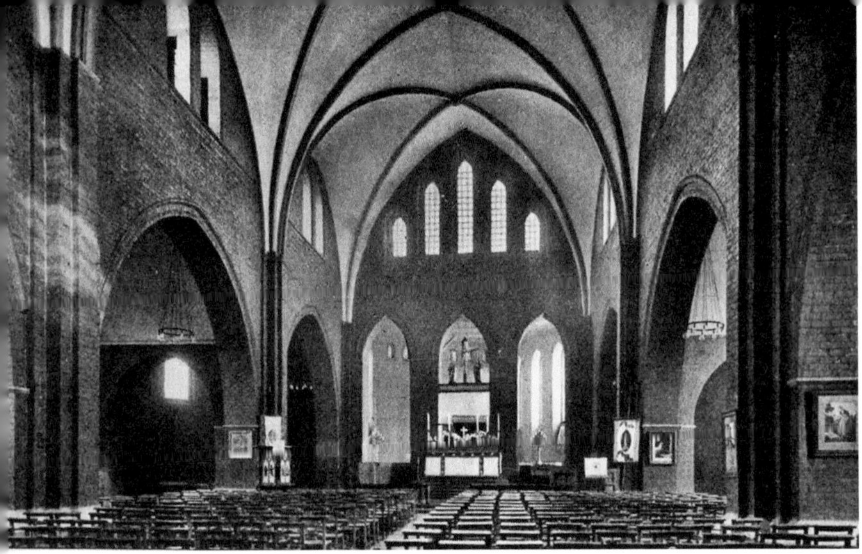

The austere interior of St Columba's Church, as illustrated in Harold Hood's *Middlesbrough Pictorial & Industrial* (1926).

The entire structure is executed in industrial red brick, producing a ruthlessly utilitarian edifice. Moore had travelled in Germany, visiting Lubeck, Stralsund and Brandenburg. He greatly admired the austere brick churches of the Baltic coast and their influence is apparent at St Columba. The composition is dominated by a massive tower that resembles a German *westwerk*, the monumental structure found at the west end of many Romanesque churches. Rising to 72 feet, the tower is asymmetrical, disrupted by the surging form of a bold stair turret. The entrance is deeply recessed within concentric brick arches. At the east end, the projecting Lady Chapel twists to the north-east to fill the angular site.

Internally, beauty could only arise from carefully judged proportions and skilful division of space. Moore turned economy into a virtue, producing an interior that is impressive in its stark efficiency. The central problem in adapting medieval plans for modern churches was the need to accommodate large congregations while ensuring that the majority had a clear view of the altar. As at St Cuthbert's, Moore opened up the church by widening the nave and reducing the side aisles to tunnel-like passages that cut through internal buttresses. He also rethought the conventional nave arcades, arguing that 'The bays of the arcades should, in my opinion, be kept fairly wide, and I think that the advantage of this is that a few large pillars do not cut up the interior of the building in the same degree as a greater number of smaller ones do.' Accordingly, Moore reduced the arcades to only three broad bays, supported on massive piers.

Echoing the exterior, the walls are of bare brick. This is the only instance in which Moore introduced exposed brick walls internally. Soaring above the nave are wooden rib vaults, a characteristic element of Moore's churches. Also typical are the arches that pierce the wall behind the altar, leading to the Lady Chapel. The central arch features a rood beam and wooden figures designed by Moore and decorated by Head & Sons in 1910. A carved, painted reredos with figures of St Columba, St Aidan, St Cuthbert and St Hilda was introduced in 1927. The Lady Chapel was dedicated as a place of worship for the local Greek Orthodox community in 1999.

Working within difficult parameters, Moore produced a building of astonishing expressive power, thoroughly appropriate for its industrial setting. With its bold massing and reinvention of traditional forms, it exemplifies Moore's modernistic Gothic architecture, which perceptive critics have interpreted as the culmination of the Gothic tradition. In a lecture to the Royal Institute of British Architects, Beresford Pite stated that 'The work of Temple Moore is rather distressing to some of us, because we cannot imagine what is to come after. It seems as if he summed up and completed the theory of the Gothic revival.'

The Albert, Albert Road (1901)

Albert Road was laid out in 1856 and although its width denotes high status, the individual plots were generally smaller than those found in other principal streets. As a result, its architecture is a panoply of different styles. Nos 38 and 40 were built as shops and offices by Sir John Fitzgerald (1857–1930), who owned a chain of public houses across the North East. The design was provided by the versatile architects James Cackett (1860–1928) and Robert Burns Dick (1868–1954), who were responsible for some of the most iconic buildings on Tyneside, including

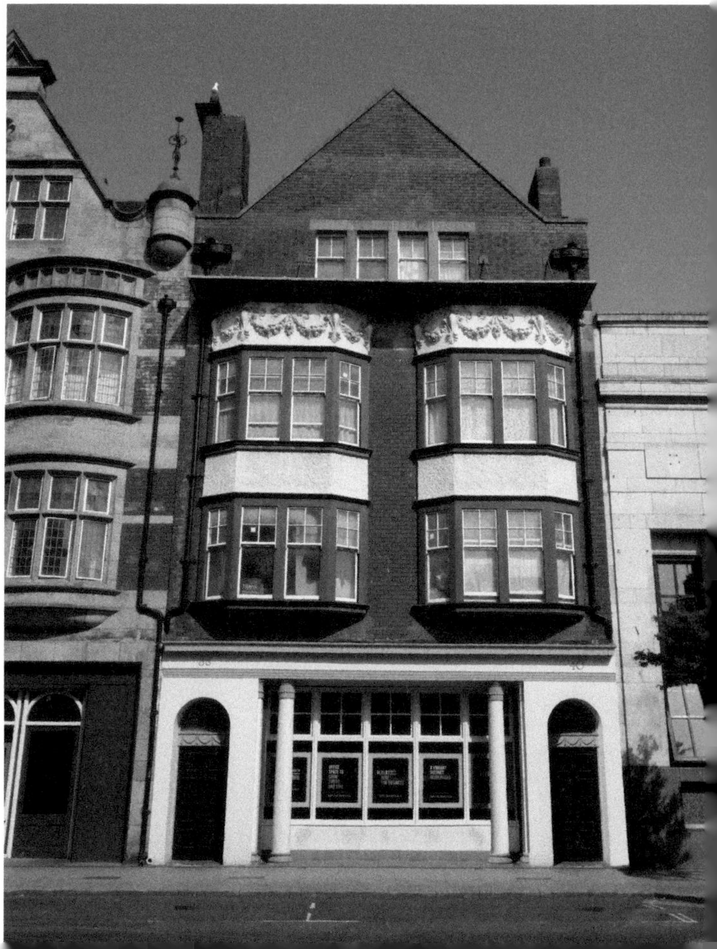

The Albert (1901), designed by Cackett and Burns Dick.

the Laing Art Gallery (1903–04) and the colossal pylons of the Tyne Bridge (1925–28). The Albert appears to be their only building in Middlesbrough and was contemporary with Newcastle's Bridge Hotel, which they designed for Fitzgerald.

The façade is built of red brick, with stone and stucco dressings. The ground floor was partly rebuilt in the mid-twentieth century and consists of a bow window recessed behind Greek columns with acanthus capitals. Twin bay windows rise through the upper floors, each boasting a frieze enriched with escutcheons and festoons. The façade ends with a plain gable, which was partially rebuilt in the twentieth century. The building is now used as a public house and is known as the Albert.

York City and County Bank, Exchange Place (1901–03)

The York City and County Bank had branches throughout Yorkshire and County Durham. Many were designed by the company's architect, W. H. Brierley. However, the Middlesbrough branch was designed by Harry Barnes (1870–1935) and Frederick E. Coates (b. 1873) of Hartlepool and Sunderland. This commercial palace is the finest work by this relatively obscure firm. In his later years, Barnes became increasingly concerned with social issues, publishing books on housing and serving as a Liberal MP for Newcastle East and as a Labour MP for East Fulham.

Occupying a prominent corner site, the building is a brilliant display of the Edwardian baroque style then in vogue, but the ornament has a sinuosity that

York City and County Bank (1901–03), exuding baroque magnificence.

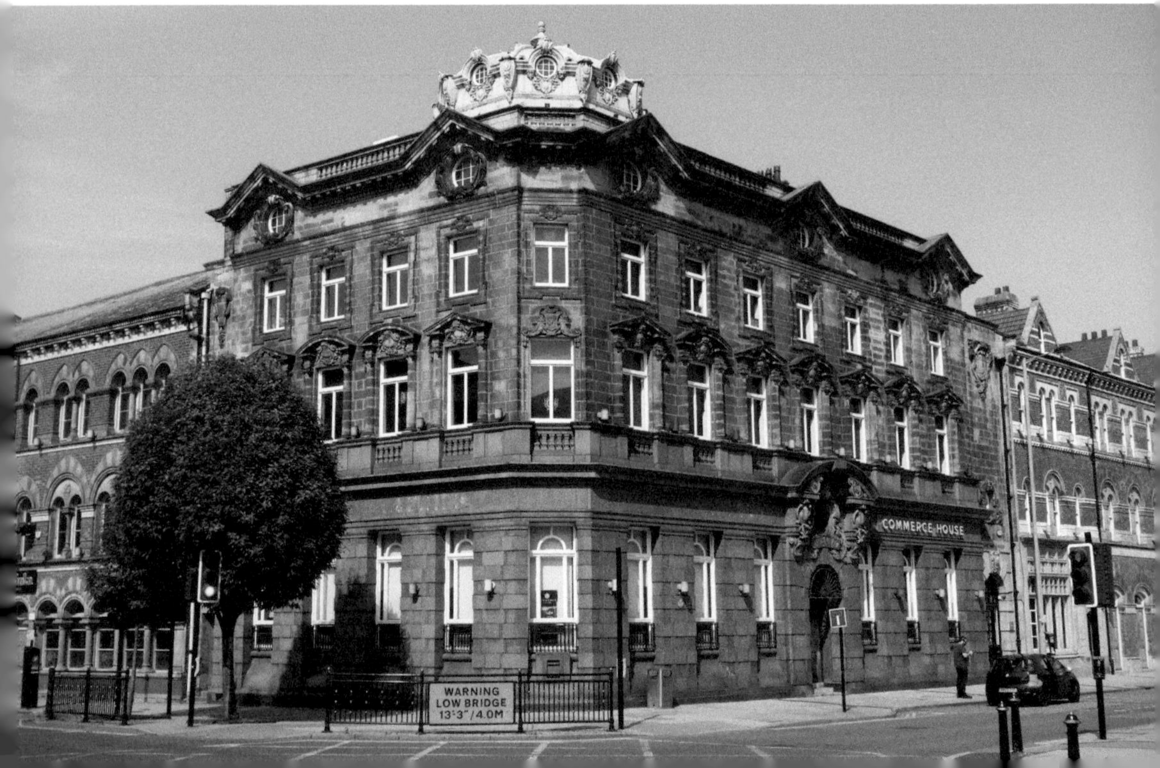

suggests the influence of Continental art nouveau. Indeed, Coates had travelled in Belgium, Germany and Russia, which would have exposed him to art nouveau and baroque influences. The ground floor is clad in polished Aberdeen granite, its hard surfaces protecting the lower reaches from damage. The entrance lies on prestigious Exchange Square, its presence announced by a glorious sculptural confection – an open segmental pediment enclosing a blind oculus, scrolled forms and escutcheons.

Contrasting with the granite base, the façades are clad in grey sandstone and studded with lavish windows, each framed by Roman Ionic columns, open pediments and escutcheons. In a strikingly original gesture, a cornice runs around the roofline, forming triangular gables over the oculus windows that pierce the attic. This curious feature is reminiscent of a detail used by Giulio Romano (*c.* 1499–1546) at his own house in Mantua (1540s), where the stringcourse forms a partial pediment over the entrance. The climax of the entire building is an exquisite octagonal lantern clad in tarnished copper with an oculus in each face. The building's interior has been refurbished, but the former banking hall featured mosaic floors and wood dado panelling with a carved cornice. An Adam-style plaster frieze with garlands of flowers ran below a geometric-patterned ceiling with fruit-and-flower ribs. This work was executed by W. & S. Wheater of Leeds.

Grand Opera House, Linthorpe Road (1903)

The area known as Swatters Carr was used for fairs and amusements, much to the annoyance of local residents, until 1900, when it was announced that an opera house was to be built at the corner of Linthorpe and Southfield Roads. The Grand Opera House was designed by William Hope (1862–1907) and Joseph Charlton Maxwell of Newcastle, who also rebuilt Middlesbrough's Theatre Royal in 1900. Hope was a prominent North East architect specialising in the design of theatres and other commercial building types. Constructed by Weldon,

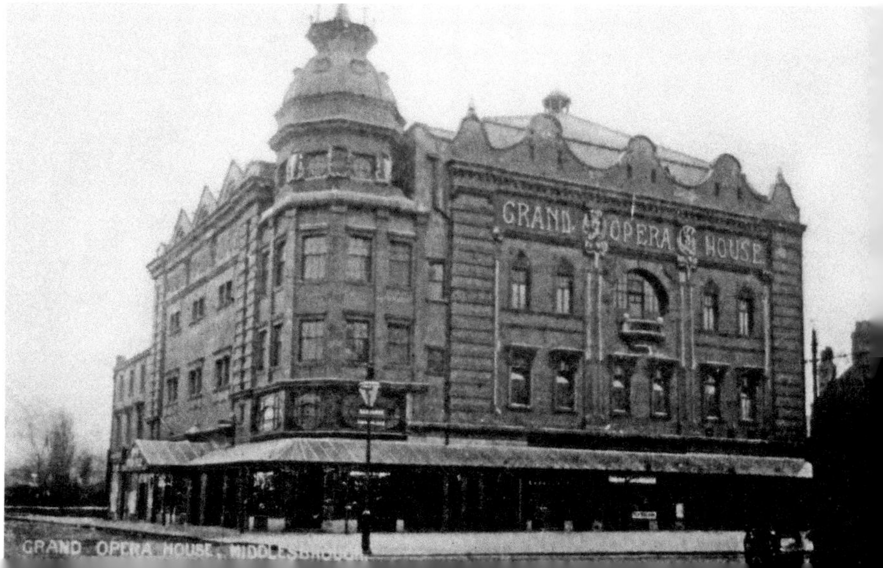

The former Grand Opera House (1903).

Watts and Company at a cost of £38,000, the Opera House was opened by S. A. Sadler MP and the mayor, Charles Dorman, on 7 December 1903.

Opera houses are typically built on a large scale in order to accommodate a grand auditorium, saloons for patrons and dressing rooms for performers. Developing a suitably aesthetic treatment for such large structures was a challenge. The design for Middlesbrough's opera house was characteristic of Hope's work, which Lynne Pearson has aptly described as 'the architecture of entertainment run riot'. The towering façades were arrayed with giant pilasters and bands of rustication made from Crombie's artificial stone, contrasting with the red Accrington brick. Series of triangular and Dutch gables crowned the façades and at the corner rose an eye-catching tower with octagonal dome and an odd metal parapet. A glass veranda covered the entrances and exits, protecting patrons from the elements as they waited for admittance.

Inside were two foyers with 'hand-painted and elaborately decorated ceilings and mosaic pavements', six cloakrooms and four saloon bars. The auditorium had capacity for 3,300 people and was lavishly decorated by A. R. Dean of Birmingham, a theatre specialist who provided furniture, marble columns and fibrous plaster ceilings. The interior was totally refurbished in 1931 and reopened as the Gaumont Palace Cinema, complete with new projection rooms, loudspeakers and a Compton organ. The cinema closed in 1964 and was eventually demolished in 1971.

Dorman Memorial Museum, Park Road (1901–04)

The Dorman Museum was a product of generous philanthropy. The steel magnate Sir A. J. Dorman offered to provide a natural history museum as a memorial to his son, Lieutenant George Lockwood Dorman, and other soldiers of the Prince of Wales's Own Yorkshire Regiment, who died in the South African War (1899–1902). The Corporation accepted this offer and appointed Dr William Young Veitch (1842–1920) as honorary curator. Veitch drew up a basic plan for the building, but the architects were J. M. Bottomley, Son and Welford of Middlesbrough and Leeds, whose design was executed at a cost of £15,000.

The Dorman Museum is an expression of the grand baroque style that was favoured during the Edwardian era. Specifically, the composition was based on a design for a house by the baroque master James Gibbs (1682–1754) and published on Plate 62 of his *Book of Architecture* (1728). This was combined with a cupola resembling those depicted on Plate 81. The principal range is a compact two-storey block crowned by a tower and octagonal cupola. The tower shown in the published plans was considerably shorter and *Building News* cryptically reported that Bottomley would 'in execution, be enabled to improve its design somewhat; but we have no further particulars'. In fact, the tower was raised during construction to give it greater prominence, but the result is a tower that is disproportionately tall in relation to the frontage.

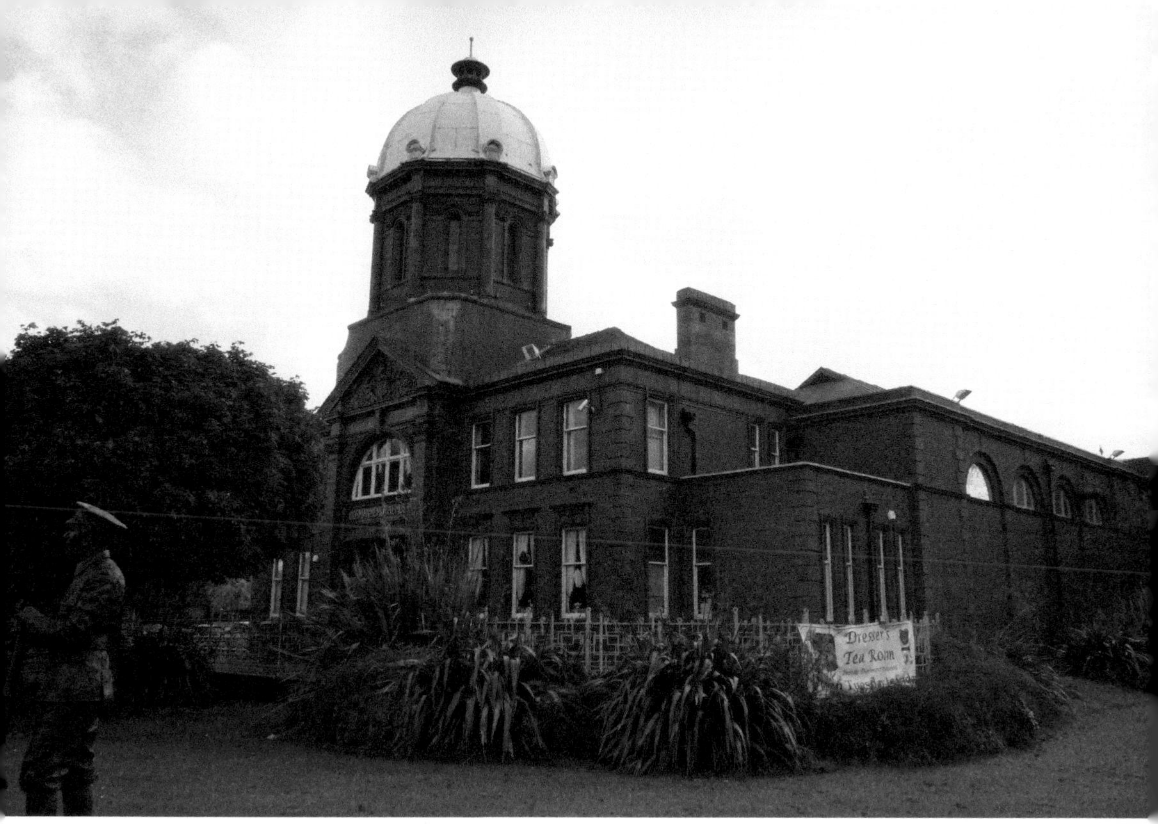

Dorman Memorial Museum (1901–04), in its armour of architectural ceramics.

The museum is executed in smooth brick, sandstone and terracotta, all with a deep red colour contrasting with the green of the tarnished copper dome. The entrance is set within a huge Ionic portico and the arms of the Borough are displayed on the tympanum. These define the building as a civic amenity, while the name 'Dorman Memorial Museum' is presented in raised lettering as a testament to its benefactor. The other faces are in plain brick, relieved only by stark pilasters, rusticated quoins and Diocletian windows derived from those used at the great bathhouses of Ancient Rome.

Internally, galleries lie to the east and west, each with barrel-vaulted roofs composed of steel ribs and purlins on stone corbels. The central gallery is lit by an octagonal umbrella dome with glazed lunettes. The use of architectural ceramics on the exterior is highly appropriate given that the museum houses a superb collection of Linthorpe pottery. In 1879, John Harrison of Darlington founded the Linthorpe Art Pottery to provide work for unemployed steelworkers. The renowned designer Christopher Dresser (1834–1904) was engaged as artistic director, in which role he produced countless exquisite designs and developed unique glazes and colour effects. Sometimes regarded as the world's first industrial designer, Dresser impressed his signature on many of these wares. He was also the first European designer to visit Japan, where he was granted access to the imperial art collections in Nara and Kyoto. In gratitude for this rare privilege, he presented a selection of Linthorpe pottery to the Japanese Meiji emperor, which is now held by the National Museum in Tokyo.

Clock and Water Tower, Dock Street (1903–04)

A prominent feature on Middlesbrough's skyline, this tower is the only remnant of the dock buildings that once served the busy coal port. Prompted by the Stockton & Darlington Railway, the Middlesbrough Owners built an enclosed dock in 1840–42 to overcome the tidal restrictions of the River Tees. A clock tower was built near the entrance lock *c.* 1846–47 to designs by the railway company's architect, John Middleton. The dock underwent three phases of expansion and remodelling during its first sixty years and the present clock tower was built following the last of these phases (1897–1902).

The tower was designed by the Architect's Department of the North Eastern Railway under William Bell, and the building contract was awarded to Thomas Dickinson & Son of West Hartlepool in 1903. The primary function of the tower was to provide the hydraulic pressure needed to operate the lock gates and other dock machinery. Two large cast-iron tanks within the body of the tower held the water and their elevation above ground level provided the necessary pressure. The structure also functioned as a clock tower, helping to regulate shift work on the docks by providing an easy way to tell the time. Finally, the soaring structure was visible out to sea and acted as a navigational aid for vessels arriving at Middlesbrough.

The multifunctional tower was built of red engineering brick but was given an aesthetic treatment with the addition of baroque details in red sandstone and terracotta. The accumulator house at the base is articulated with tall,

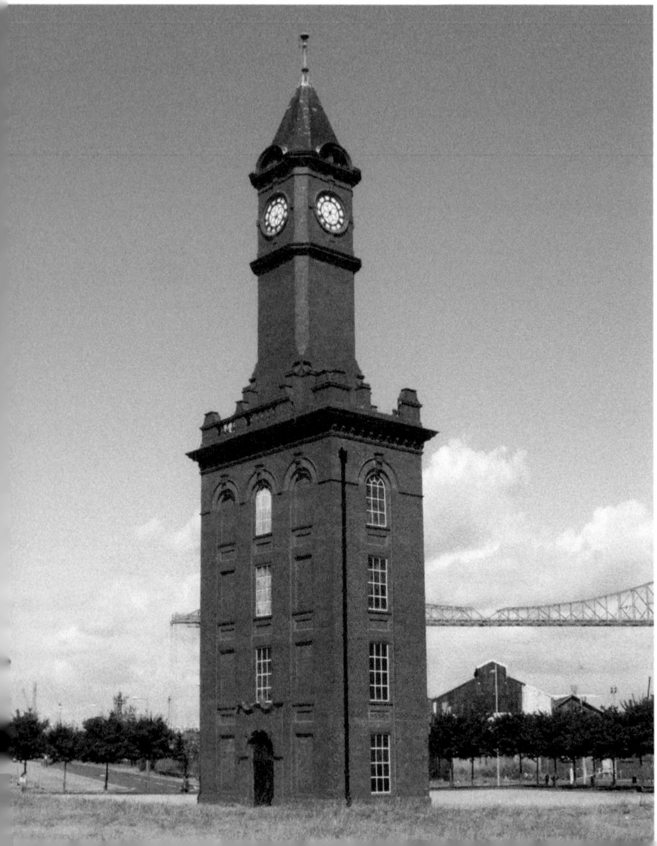

The former Clock and Water Tower of Middlesbrough Docks (1903–04).

arched recesses and crowned with an ornamental parapet. The clock tower rises from the base and ends in a pyramidal roof, much like the tower Bell designed for Darlington's Bank Top Station (1887). The construction costs were £805 for the accumulator house, excluding the tanks and machinery, and £542 for the upper tower and clock, which was provided by Potts of Leeds, the usual suppliers to the North Eastern Railway.

The new dock offices, also designed by Bell, consisted of a four-storey building in red brick. Extensive terracotta ornament was provided by the renowned firm of Burmantofts of Leeds. When Britain's railways were nationalised in 1948, the dock and railway were separated, and the office building was eventually demolished.

Park Methodist Church, Linthorpe Road (1903–05)

Park Methodist Church was built by Middlesbrough's Wesleyan congregation at a cost of £10,000. The rich Italianate design by W. J. Morley & Son of Bradford illustrates how far Methodism had developed from a traditionally working-class faith espousing modesty and restraint. By the early twentieth century, Methodist sects had erected elaborate churches in every major architectural style, reflecting the growing social status of their congregations. Churches in the Italian Renaissance style are rare in the North East, but Park Methodist Church is one of several examples in Middlesbrough.

Park Methodist Church (1903–05), an homage to Renaissance churches.

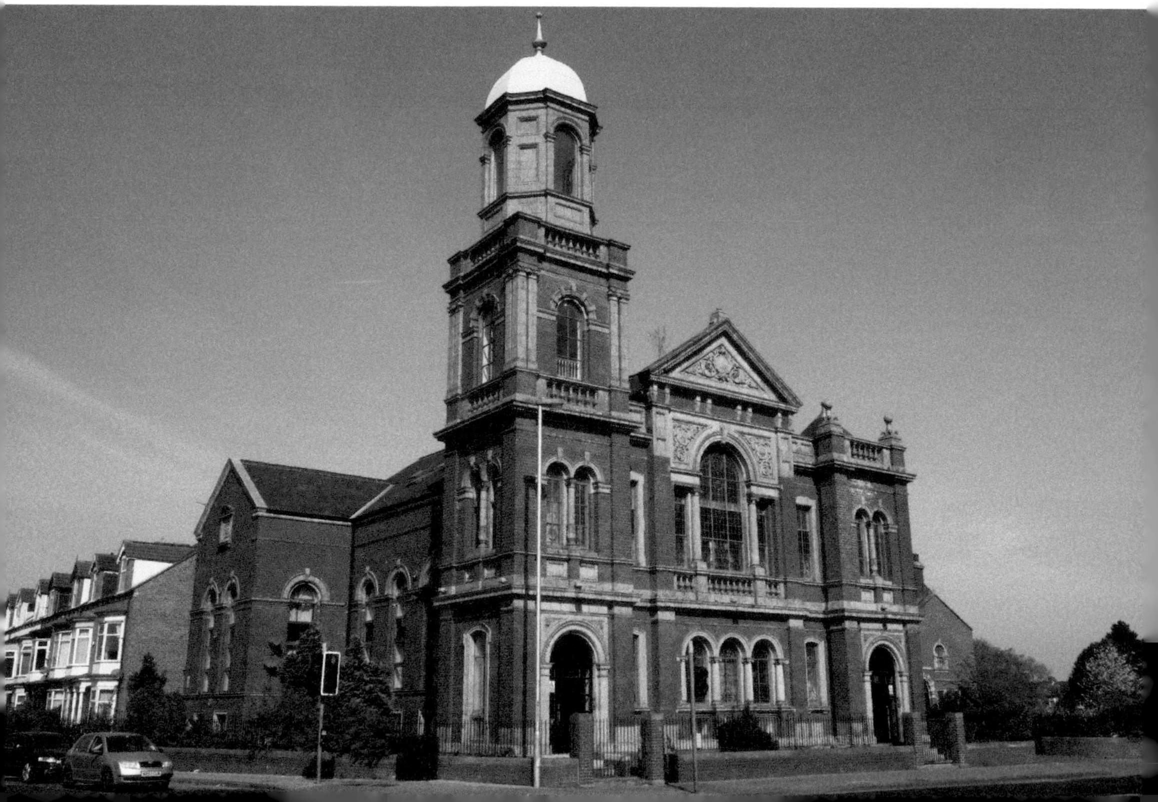

In order to give the church an imposing frontage to Linthorpe Road, it was positioned in reverse of the traditional east-west orientation. The nave is flanked by towers, one of which supports an octagonal cupola and copper dome. It is possible that the second tower was intended to repeat this design, giving the church a symmetrical frontage, but if so, it was never completed. A splendid Venetian window fills the central gable, with swirling ornament in the spandrels. The interior, seating 700, boasted a plaster chancel arch, panelled ceiling and a tessellated floor. No longer used for worship, the building has been converted into apartments, which has safeguarded the exterior, but destroyed much of the original interior.

Maritime Buildings, Albert Road (1905)

The former Trustee Savings Bank on Albert Road is a delightful addition to a richly varied streetscape. Like the earlier Forbes Building, it illustrates Roger Lofthouse's lightness of touch in the design of commercial buildings and uses the same materials of red brick and golden sandstone. Shallow bay windows enliven the façade and a triangular gable draws the composition together. No doubt the gable was introduced to complement that of the neighbouring building, designed by Cackett and Burns Dick. Charming features are the tiny bartizans, or overhanging turrets, capped with ornate iron finials.

The design is characteristic of the English Domestic Revival, a movement that drew inspiration from traditional domestic architecture. In particular, the chromatic effect of brick and stone recalls Norman Shaw's celebrated design for

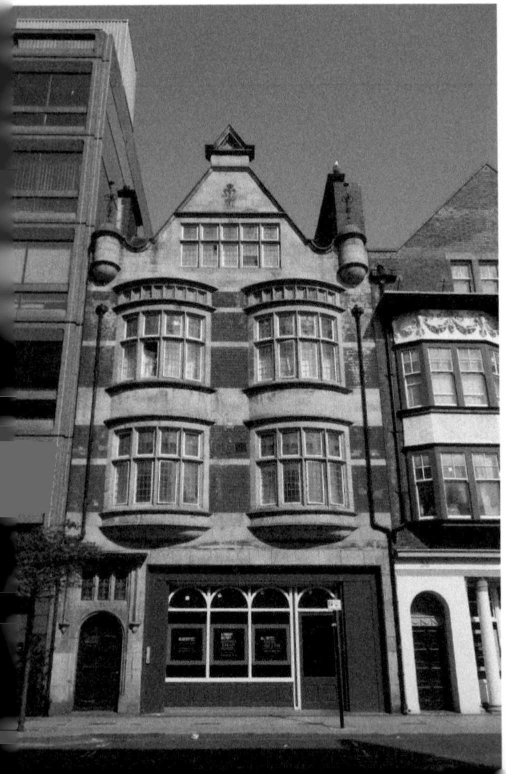

Maritime Buildings (1905), formerly a Trustee Savings Bank.

Scotland Yard, as do the bartizans. There is also a clear influence from art nouveau in the stained-glass windows, which emulate Charles Rennie Mackintosh's stylised rose motifs. Reportedly, the first-floor front room retains a Jacobean-style plaster ceiling, wooden dado panelling and original fireplaces.

Nazareth House, Park Road North (1905–06)

This former children's home was one of many such institutions established by the Poor Sisters of Nazareth, a community of Roman Catholic nuns founded by Victoire Larmenier in 1857. These institutions were known as Nazareth Houses and provided accommodation for destitute children. A Nazareth House was established in Middlesbrough in 1880, located at Albert Park Road. The present, larger, building was erected in 1905–06 to designs by Edward Goldie of London, the son of prolific Catholic architect George Goldie. A chapel was added in 1894, designed by Henry Weatherill, architect to Stockton School Board, and E. A. Whipham.

Nazareth House was designed in the Queen Anne style, an informal derivative of classicism loosely based on the architecture of the Queen Anne period (1702–14). Characteristic of the style are the red-brick façades, stone detailing and white-painted sash windows. In contrast to the more dogmatic Gothic Revival, these elements gave the building a domestic character appropriate for a children's home. The three central bays are surmounted by a classical pediment. The main door is framed by columns with waterleaf capitals and a graceful segmental pediment. A tiered strip of masonry rises from the entrance to the crowning gable and forms a niche containing a statue of the Virgin and Child. Maximising the internal space, an attic storey is housed within the hipped roof, lit by dormer windows with

The Queen Anne-style façade of Nazareth House (1905–06).

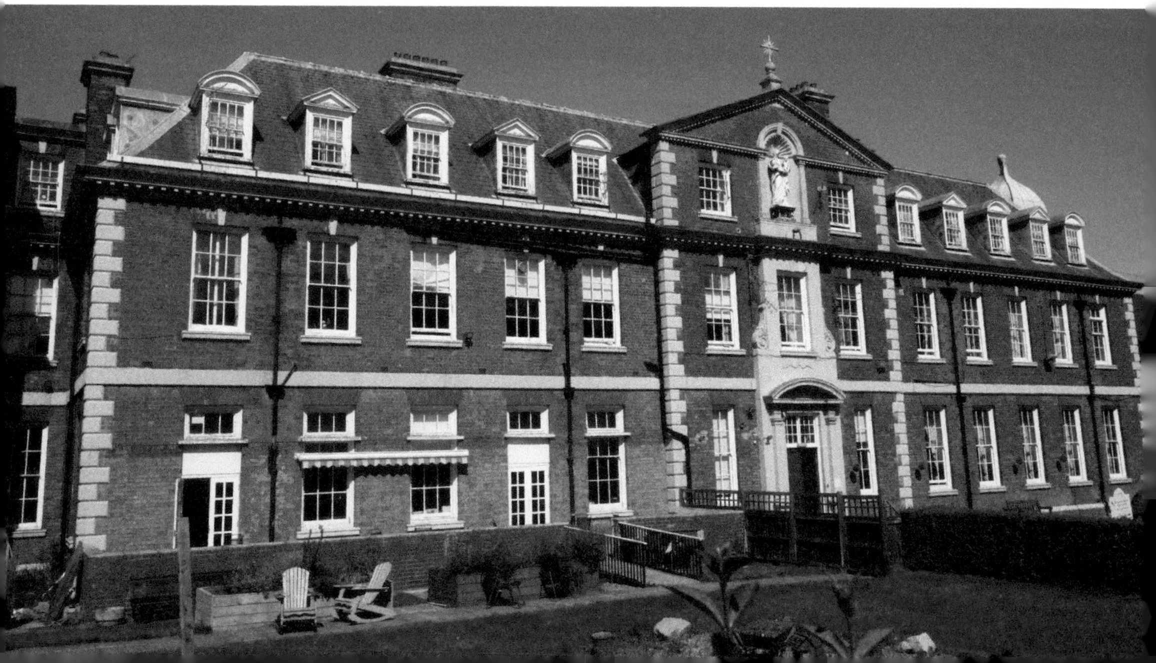

alternating triangular and segmental pediments. While the building exudes the 'sweetness and light' typical of the Queen Anne style, it belied what was by many accounts a harsh regime. Nazareth House closed as a children's home in 2007 and the building is now used as a home for the elderly.

Central Public Library, Victoria Square (1909–12)

The Scottish-American industrialist Sir Andrew Carnegie funded the building of hundreds of public libraries throughout the world. In January 1908, he announced that he would donate £15,000 for a new library in Middlesbrough. Land was offered by Sir Hugh Bell and Alderman Amos Hinton. Built by Henry McNaughton of Middlesbrough, the library cost £16,423 *6s. 10d.* Carnegie agreed to pay half of the excess, providing that the remainder was made up by public subscription. This was the largest Carnegie library in the North East, perhaps because, as a steel magnate, Carnegie had a vested interest in securing good relations with Middlesbrough, a world-leading centre of steel production.

The Central Public Library was designed by Samuel Bridgman Russell (1864–1955) and Sir Thomas Edwin Cooper (1874–1942) in an institutional Edwardian classical style. Born in Scarborough, Cooper had been an assistant to W. H. Brierley and Goldie, Child and Goldie in York. He established independent practice in 1893, with offices in Scarborough and Westminster, but soon formed a partnership with Russell, which lasted until 1912.

Although adapted to Edwardian taste, the building's classical elements allude to Greek and Roman civilisation, defining the library as a temple of knowledge.

Central Public Library (1909–12), funded by Andrew Carnegie.

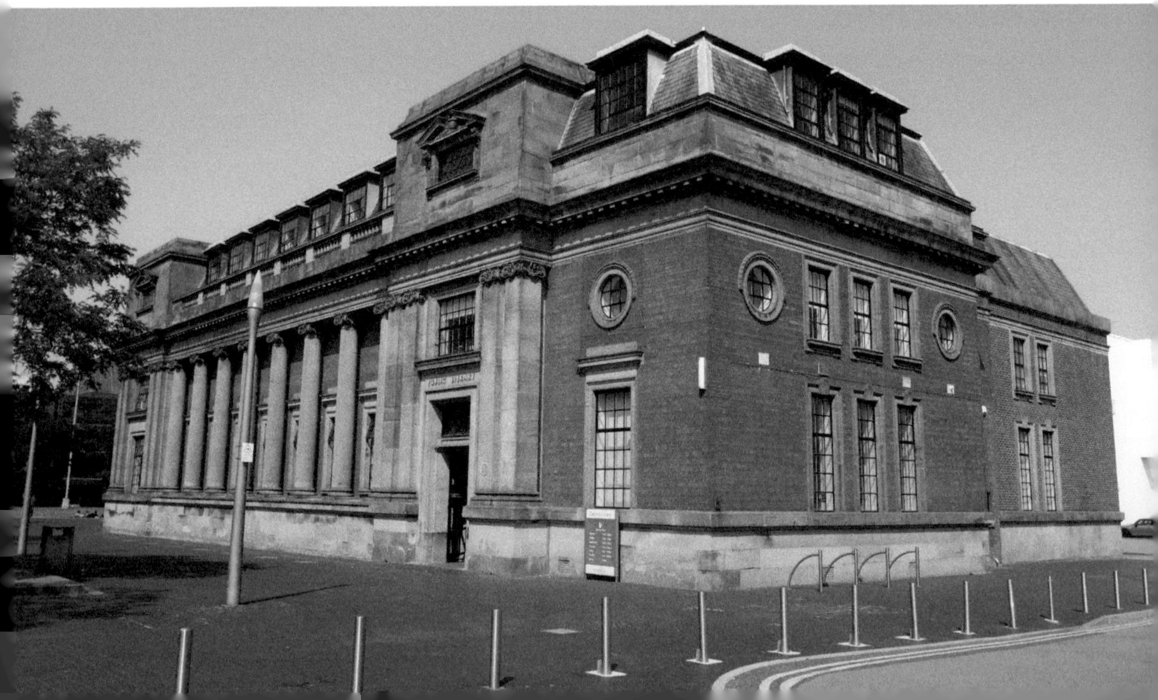

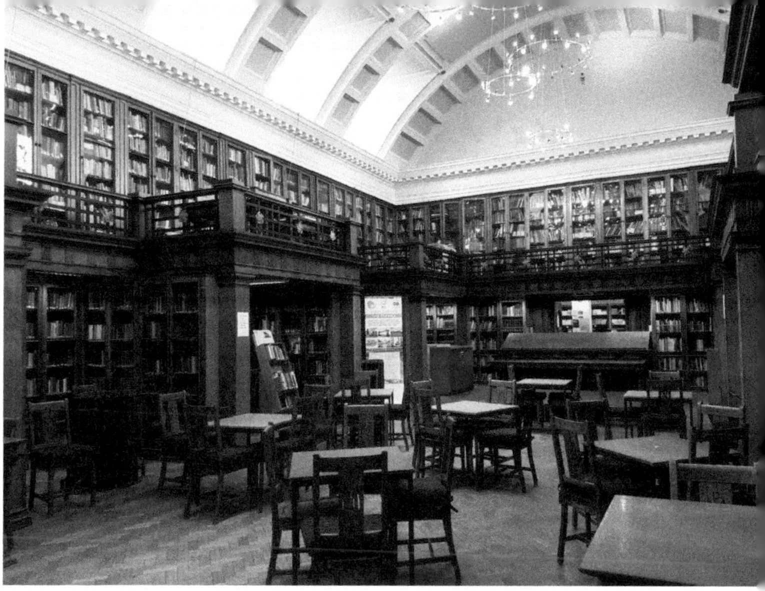

The fine interior of the reference library.

The body is symmetrical, with twin pavilions flanking a seven-bay colonnade of giant Ionic columns. A deep continuous plinth and heavy entablature give the building a powerful horizontal emphasis. Accentuating the composition is a simple, but effective byplay between red brick and sandstone. The entrance hall is clad in marble and an imperial staircase leads to the first-floor reference library, which features a segmental-arched ceiling. Oak-panelled walls and a continuous gallery supported on Roman Doric columns make this one of Middlesbrough's finest historic interiors. The original furniture was designed by Cooper, in consultation with the Borough Librarian.

Tees Transporter Bridge (1909–11)

Without doubt the most iconic structure in Middlesbrough, the Tees Transporter Bridge was built to replace the ferries that carried workers between the factories and foundries of Middlesbrough and Port Clarence. Opened in 1911, the innovative structure transported iron and steel workers across the Tees without impeding traffic on this vital industrial artery. Fewer than twenty transporter bridges have ever been built across the globe. Middlesbrough's bridge is the largest of its kind in the world and one of only two such bridges still operating in Britain.

The idea of a bridge incorporating an aerial ferry had been suggested as early as 1872 by Charles Smith, manager of the Hartlepool Iron Works. However, the concept was patented by French engineer Ferdinand Joseph Arnodin and Spaniard Martin Alberto Palacio in 1887. Of the eighteen transporter bridges ever built, nine can be attributed to Arnodin.

Proposals to erect a transporter bridge over the Tees resurfaced in 1905. The Board of Trade appointed London engineer A. G. Pain to draw up a report and in October 1906 it was decided to proceed with construction. After consulting Arnodin, the Corporation met with William Edwin Pease (1865–1926), chairman of the Cleveland Bridge & Engineering Company, and its chief engineer,

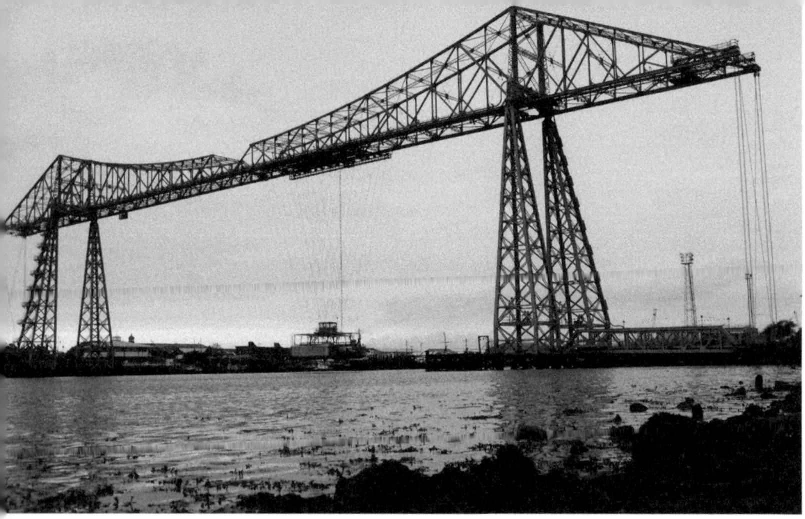

Transporter Bridge (1909–11). (James T. M. Towill/ CC BY–SA 2.0)

Georges Camille Imbault (1877–1951), who had worked on Arnodin's bridges in Tunisia and Rouen. Imbault and the Cleveland Bridge & Engineering Company were appointed to design the structure and the contract for its construction was awarded to famed bridge builders Sir William Arrol & Company of Glasgow, whose tender for the work was £68,026 *6s. 8d.* The resident engineer was R. Anderson, assisted by Borough Engineer Samuel Edwin Burgess (b. 1863), who was also qualified as an architect. The electrical work was supervised by the Borough Electrical Engineer, H. M. Taylor. The total cost of the bridge was £87,316 13*s.* 8*d.*

The resulting steel truss bridge is a mammoth structure supported on two pairs of tapering steel lattice towers. Built on a cantilever principle, the ends are tethered to the ground with steel cables anchored in concrete. The bridge's moving platform or 'gondola' is suspended by cables from a trolley running on rails along the gantry, powered electrically from a winding house on the Middlesbrough side. Dominating the skyline, the heroic structure is 850 feet long, with a central span of 590 feet, and 223 feet high.

With the industrial decline of the 1970s, the bridge was threatened with demolition, but it has entered the new millennium as a symbol of Middlesbrough's industrial and engineering heritage. The bridge underwent extensive refurbishment in 2011, aided by £2.6m from the Heritage Lottery Fund to mark its centenary. The transformation included state-of-the-art visitor facilities and a glass viewing lift to provide access to the upper walkway. The celebrated landmark remains an icon of Middlesbrough and a monument to its world-renowned steel industry.

Shakespeare Public House, Linthorpe Road (1911)

In its early days, the population of Middlesbrough consisted mainly of male industrial workers and it was not long before public houses were opened to capitalise on their need for leisure facilities and respite from physical labour. The Shakespeare was built as a public house in the mid-nineteenth century,

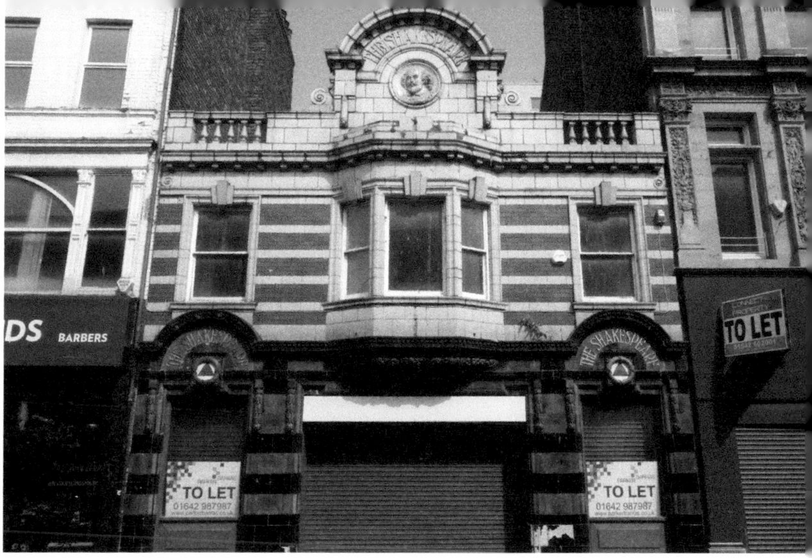

The renewed façade of the Shakespeare Public House (1911).

originally to a less elaborate design. The building was given a fashionable new frontage by Robert Ridley Kitching (1877–1954) and William Winder Lee (b. 1873) in 1911. One of Middlesbrough's most prominent architects, Kitching established practice in Durham in 1900. He was joined in partnership by Richard Archibald in 1904 and then in 1905 by William Lee. In 1930, he formed a partnership with Lewis Wade and Jack Rudd, renaming the practice Kitching & Co.

The ground floor has a glistening fascia in vibrant green faience, while the upper storey is lined with red brick and gleaming white terracotta. The details are classical but have a crispness typical of the early twentieth century, when a number of architects attempted to modernise the classical style.

An oriel window dominates the façade, beneath a splendid Dutch gable decorated with volutes (scrolls) and fasces, or bundles of rods, a Roman symbol for power and authority. The name of the pub is proudly displayed across each of its three pediments and there is a relief portrait of William Shakespeare under the main gable. Similarly, the logo of the Bass brewery, Britain's first registered trademark, is displayed within curious lifebelt motifs.

Masham Hotel, Linthorpe Road (1913–14)

The Masham Hotel was built in the mid-nineteenth century as a modest two-storey building. The façade is covered with roughcast, scored to imitate masonry, and there is rudimentary classical ornament in the form of vermiculated quoins (cornerstones decorated with irregular grooves resembling worm-tracks). In 1913–14, the building was given a spectacular new frontage by architects Kitching and Lee of Middlesbrough.

The ground floor was clad with faience tiles in a lavish baroque style and iridescent green colour. Faience, a tin-glazed architectural ceramic, had been popular since the 1880s, particularly for commercial buildings such as public houses. The fact that it was mass-produced in modular components made

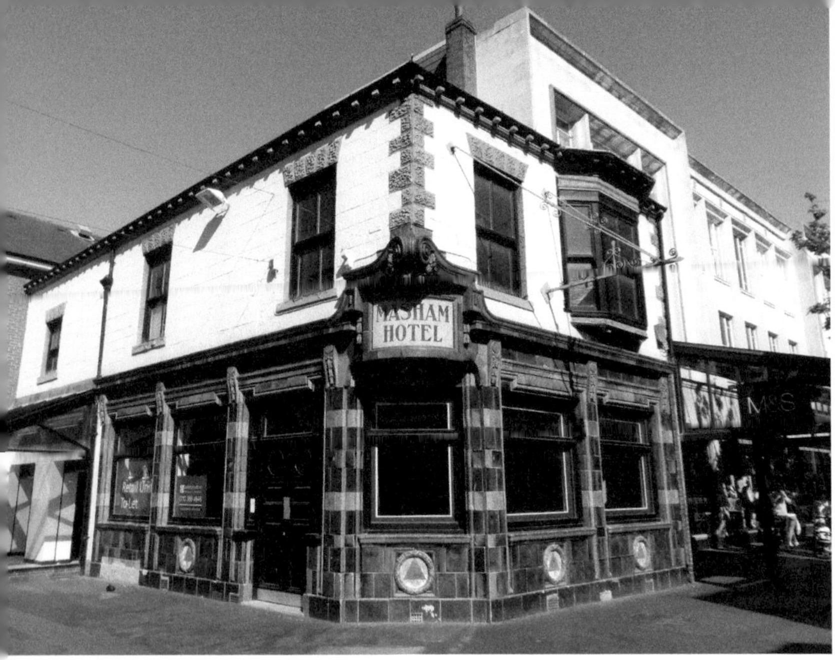

Vibrant faience tiles at the Masham Hotel (1913–14).

it economical, while the eye-catching colour and ornate detail were ideal for attracting customers. These decorative surfaces culminate in a mosaic panel above the entrance, displaying the name of the pub beneath an elaborate scrolled form. The logo of the Bass brewery, a red triangle, is displayed beneath the windows.

London City and Midland Bank, Linthorpe Road (1912)

Forming a splendid set-piece at the junction of Linthorpe and Borough Roads, this inventive building was designed by Thomas Bostock Whinney (1860–1926) and James Forbes (1880–1925) for the London City and Midland Bank. Born in London, Whinney studied at the Royal Academy schools and travelled in France and Italy, before accepting a post as architect to the London City

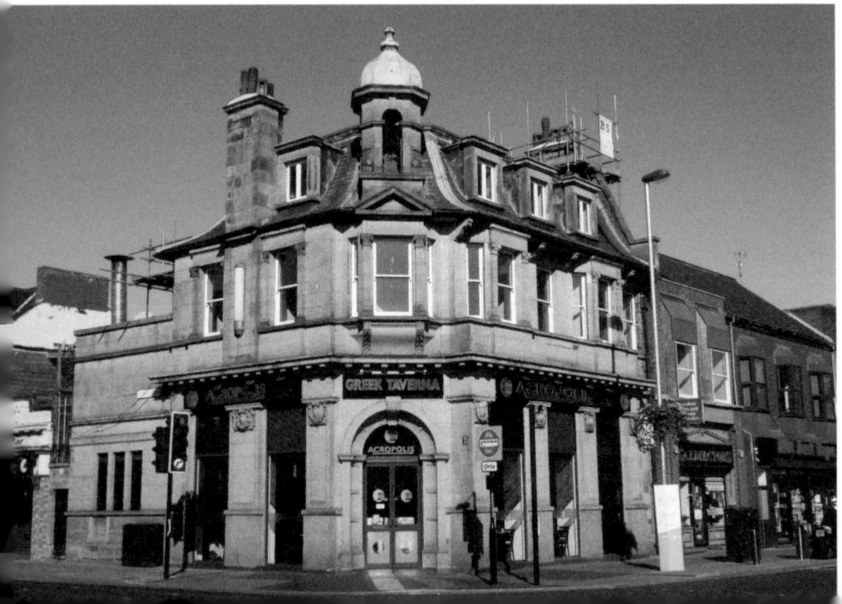

London City and Midland Bank (1912), in Edwardian classical style.

and Midland Bank. Forbes studied at Middlesbrough High School and was articled to local architects Roger Lofthouse and Sons. He was an assistant in London County Council's Architects' Department in 1903–05, before returning to Middlesbrough, where he designed several schools as well as other building types.

The design is typical of the branches Whinney designed for the firm, resembling that in Newport, Wales (1896–97). Characteristic are the canted corner entrance, oriel window and eye-catching octagonal lantern, as well as the hipped roof broken by dormers. The bank was designed in an Edwardian classical style, rather than the more grandiose baroque style that was in vogue in this period. Although rather severe in its parts, the composition is a spirited interplay of masses and voids. Strong pilasters on the ground floor are ornamented with cartouches.

Freeman, Hardy and Willis, Corporation Road (1912–13)

This fine commercial building comprising Nos 29 and 31 Corporation Road and No. 65 Albert Road was built for Freeman, Hardy and Willis Ltd, a shoe retailer established in 1875. Built of brick and faced in buff terracotta, the premises incorporated a shop and hotel. The design, by Moore and Archibald of Middlesbrough, illustrates the transition between the Edwardian grand manner and the 'stripped classicism' of the 1920s.

Freeman, Hardy and Willis (1912–13), lacking its original attic storey.

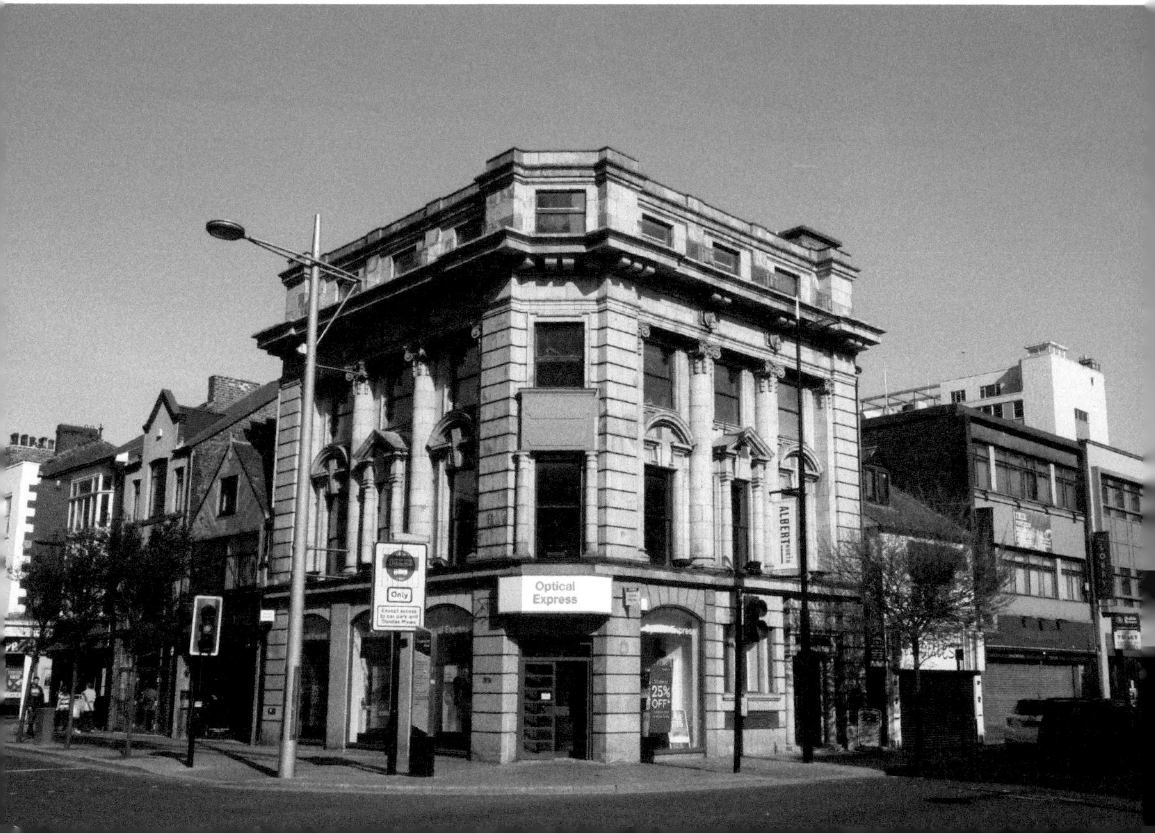

The corner is canted to form an entrance and focal point. The walls are scaled by giant Ionic columns, executed in a modernistic manner and indented into the façades, supporting a heavy entablature. The remaining surfaces are rusticated to convey an effect of strength. Treated as a *piano nobile*, the first floor is emphasised by elaborate windows with triangular and segmental pediments and exaggerated keystones. In its materials and motifs, the building was probably influenced by the renewed frontage of Fenwick's department store in Newcastle (1913). The building was altered *c.* 1980 when an attic storey incorporating dormers and ornamental chimney stacks was removed.

Crown Building, Linthorpe Road (1919–23)

This former entertainment venue was built as the Elite Cinema in 1919–23, one of several picture palaces owned by Walter Bentley Cinemas Ltd. The building was designed by architect James Forbes, who succeeded in devising a stately and carefully modulated composition despite its large scale. In its details, the building reflects the stripped classical style of the 1920s, but the massing, with a cylindrical corner tower and ziggurat roofline, anticipates the art deco 'dream palaces' of the 1930s. The building's principal faces are symmetrical, joined by the imposing corner drum. Arrayed with pilasters and demi-lune windows, these façades enclose the former auditorium, which was crowned by a shallow domed roof.

Crown Building (1919–23), marking the transition from stripped classicism to art deco.

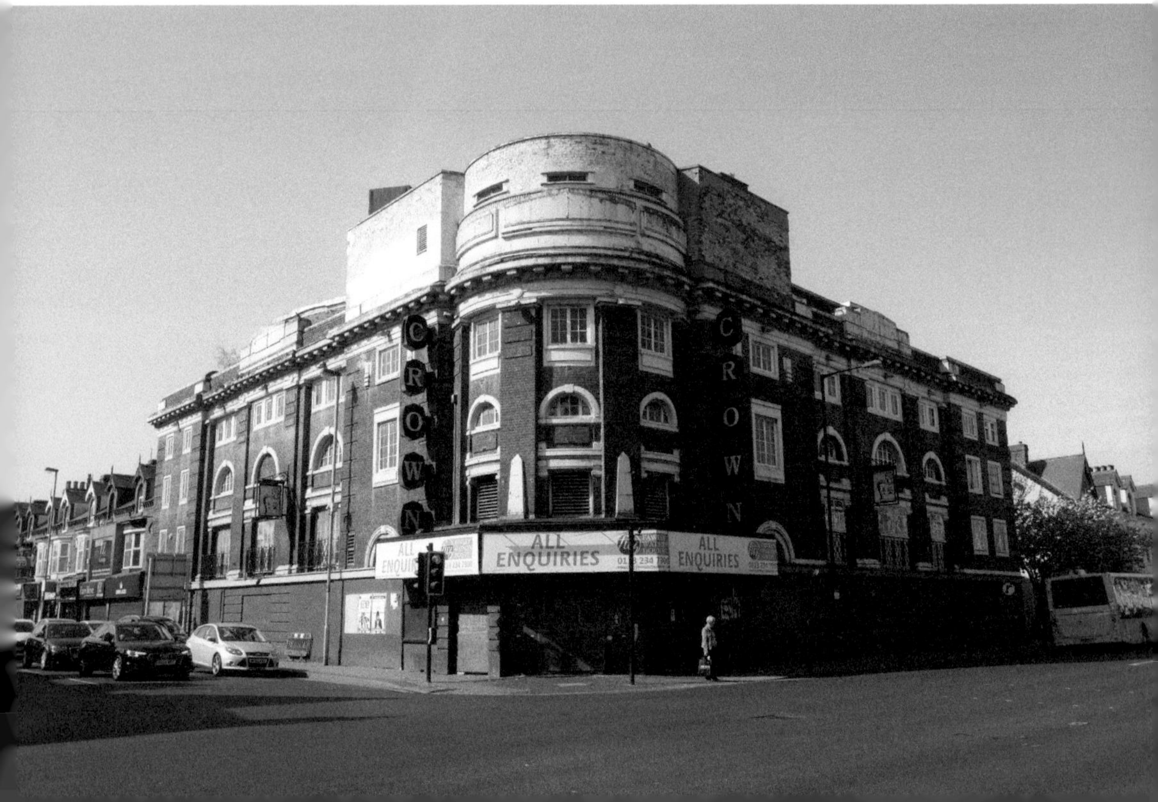

The presence of Egyptian obelisks above the entrance illustrates the craze of Egyptomania that swept the world following the discovery of Tutankhamun's tomb in 1922.

Besides a 1,900-seat auditorium, the cinema boasted a stage and a café with space for dancing. A Compton organ and Western Electric sound system were installed in 1930. The building was taken over by Associated British Cinemas in 1935 and modernised in 1964, when it was renamed the ABC. The building became the Crown Bingo Club in 1987 but was converted into a pub in 1996. The pub closed in 2015 and various plans have since been suggested for regenerating the building.

Park Presbyterian Church, Linthorpe Road (1923–24)

A Presbyterian community developed in Middlesbrough as Scottish migrants came seeking work in its thriving industries. A church was built in Newport Road in 1864–65, designed by W. H. Blessley, but as the town continued to expand, a second place of worship was opened on Linthorpe Road. Park Presbyterian Church was built by Stephen Coates Ltd. Donors included the shipbuilder Sir Robert A. Bartram, who also funded a Presbyterian church in Sunderland.

Although the site was somewhat restricted, the architects, Archibald and Kitching, were able to achieve a traditional plan, with nave, aisles, porch and transepts.

Park Presbyterian Church (1923–24), with its sparkling frontage.

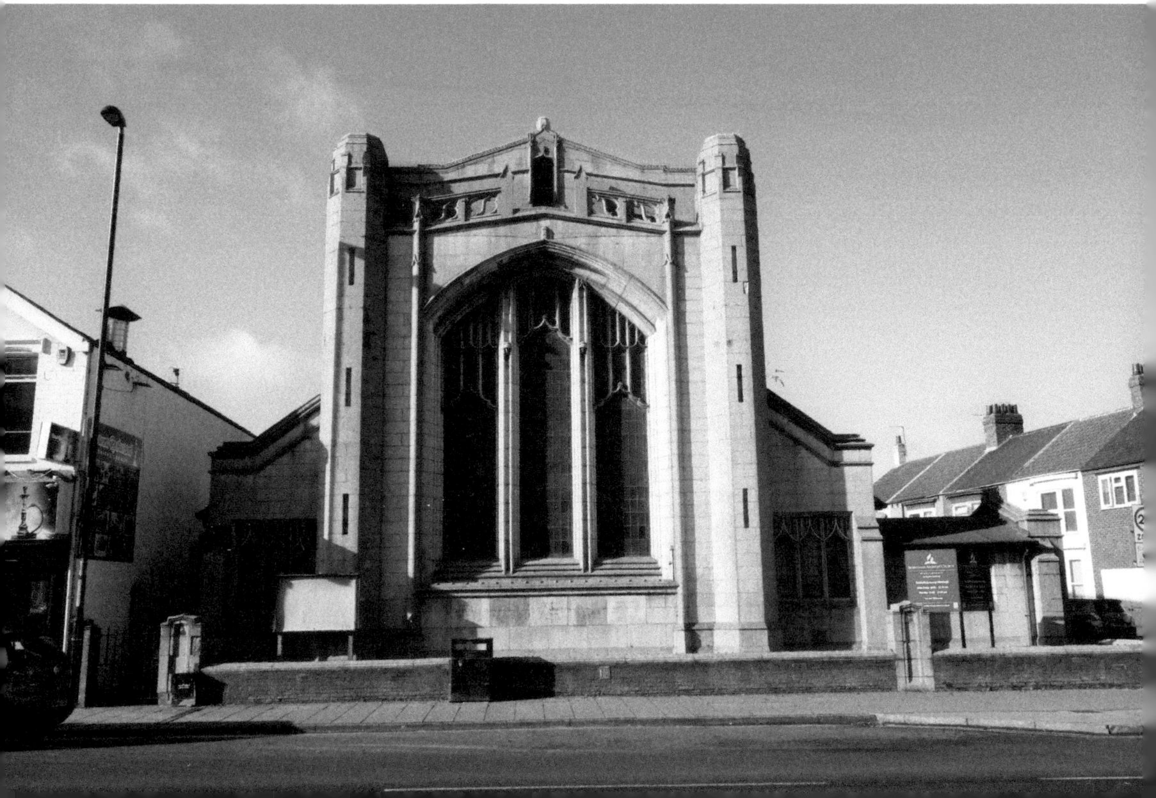

Architectural display is concentrated in the Linthorpe Road frontage, which is clad in artificial stone made to look like sparkling grey granite to evoke the Scottish origins of Presbyterianism. The other faces are predominately built of cheaper brick. Designed in a bold Gothic style, the church is a very late example of medievalism, but the architects made a clear effort to adapt the style for the twentieth century. The great west window translates the Perpendicular Gothic tracery of *c.* 1350–1520 into modernistic terms and the octagonal towers that delineate the façade anticipate the art deco style that Kitching would use to spectacular effect at Ralph Sparks' Daylight Bakery in 1938. The building is now used as a Seventh Day Adventist church.

First Church of Christ Scientist, Southfield Road (1927)

This diminutive building was the only purpose-built Christian Science church in the North East. Founded in New England in the nineteenth century, the Christian Science movement is based on a system of religious psychotherapeutics developed by Mary Baker Eddy, whose book *Science and Health* (1875) asserts that sickness can be cured by prayer alone. A Middlesbrough church was established in the home of Alfred Edwards, a former Member of Parliament. Sessions were held in various locations until a permanent church was built in Southfield Road.

Designed by Borough Engineer S. E. Burgess, who was himself a member of the sect, the building exhibited an American neoclassical style typical of New England, thus introducing yet another style to Middlesbrough's ecclesiastical architecture. The design consisted of twin pavilions connected by a simple tetrastyle portico, leading into a central prayer hall. These low volumes were executed in brick and white stucco, in common with American examples such as the Christian Science church at Quincy, Illinois (1910).

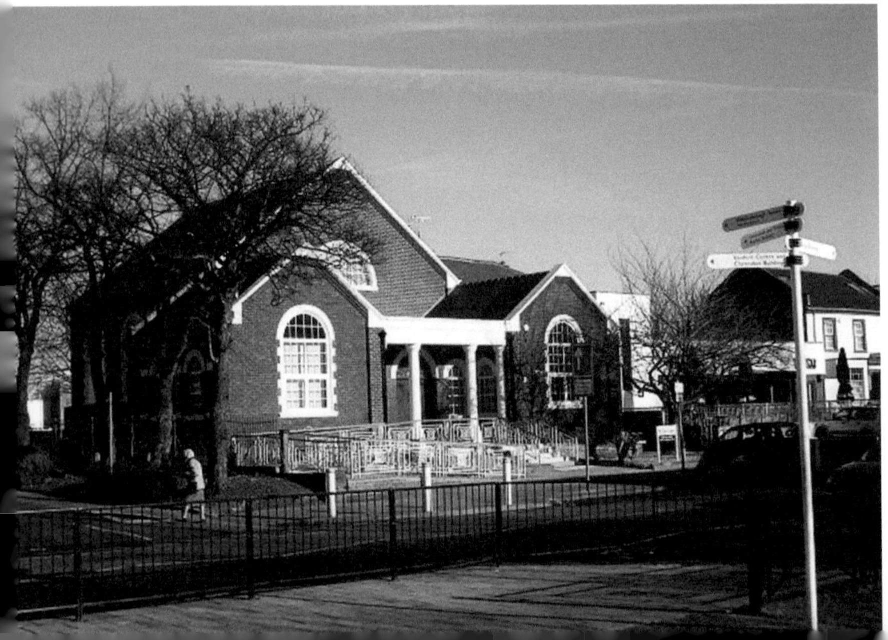

First Church of Christ Scientist (1927). (Ian Stubbs)

In recent decades, the building was used by Teesside University for administration purposes but was demolished to make way for a £12.5m Student Life Building. The loss of this charming and unique structure exemplifies the incremental erosion of Middlesbrough's heritage.

Constantine Building, Borough Road (1929–30)

As a major industrial centre, Middlesbrough needed facilities for technical education. In 1913, a technical college and art school were proposed for a site in Borough Road, which had been procured by Sir Hugh Bell. Local shipping magnate Joseph Constantine (1856–1922) offered a contribution of £40,000 in 1916, stating that technical education was vital if Britain was to compete with other nations, particularly Germany. This was followed by pledges from Dorman Long and others. The First World War delayed development until 1924, but by this time the projected costs had risen to £80,000. Fortunately, Constantine's widow and family provided the remaining finances.

The Constantine Building was designed by Graham Richards Dawbarn (1893–1976), an architect best known for his modernist design for BBC Television Centre in London (1949–60). Construction was carried out by the prolific Newcastle builder Stephen Easten. The structure is built on an epic scale in a proto-modernist style. This, and the machinic precision of the masonry in white Portland stone, emphasises the college's technical focus.

The plan is actually E-shaped, but the imposing façades give the impression of a foursquare edifice. The building stands on a granite plinth and boasts a marble and granite door surround of uncompromising severity. The fenestration follows an unrelenting rhythm and each window is recessed within a shallow portal with the starkest of ornamentation. A Welsh-slate roof completes the design, its deeply overhanging eaves resting on curved brackets. Constantine College became a polytechnic in 1969, eventually forming the nucleus of Teesside University.

Constantine Building (1929–30). (Middlesbrough Libraries and Information)

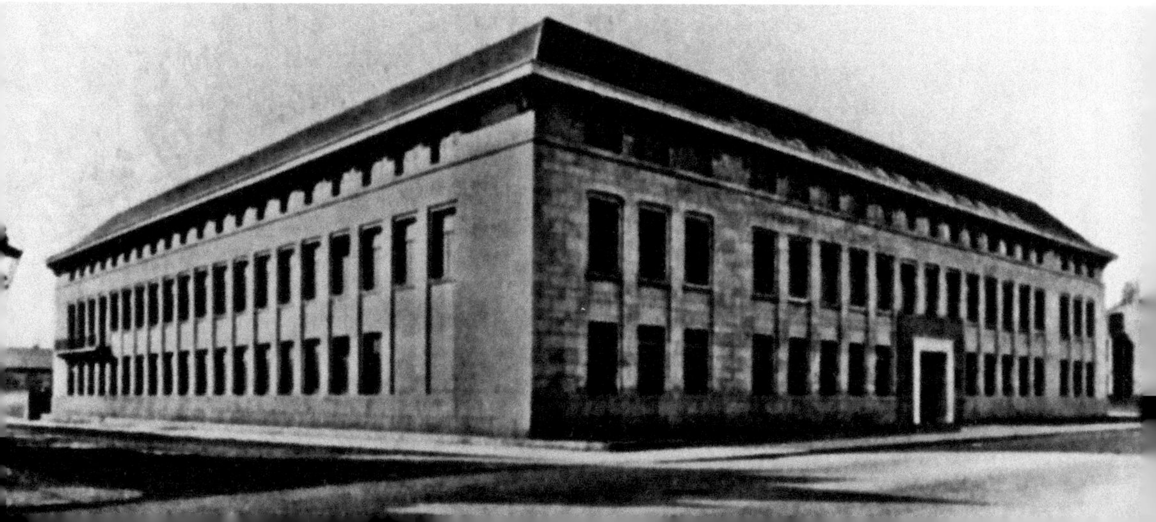

Church of the Sacred Heart, Linthorpe Road (1930–32)

Standing resplendent on Linthorpe Road, the Roman Catholic Church of the Sacred Heart is the jewel of Middlesbrough's religious architecture. Inspired by the Romanesque churches of Flanders and decorated with luminous mosaics, its design was unique in the North East, although it inspired several imitations. The church was originally dedicated to the Sacred Heart of Jesus and St Philomena but has been known as the Sacred Heart Church since the 1960s.

Unmistakably European in conception, the building was designed by Belgian architect Jules Coomans (1871–1937) of Ypres, with assistance from local architects Kitching & Co. After the death of his parents, Coomans became a ward of his uncle, a Catholic monk. He studied engineering architecture at the Catholic University of Leuven and worked as City Architect for Ypres from 1895 to 1931. In this role, he was principally responsible for the city's reconstruction after the First World War. The Sacred Heart was loosely modelled on the Benedictine abbey of Saint Andrew near Bruges (1899–1900). The Flemish design helped to distinguish the building from Anglican churches.

The plan is cruciform, with short transepts and a dodecagonal apse at the east end. The body is built of Belgian yellow brick, with dressings of white Portland stone and terracotta flowers to enrich the colour palette. The eaves have stepped brick corbelling. Two towers loom over Linthorpe Road, their upper stages

Church of the Sacred Heart (1930–32), introducing Flemish Romanesque to Middlesbrough.

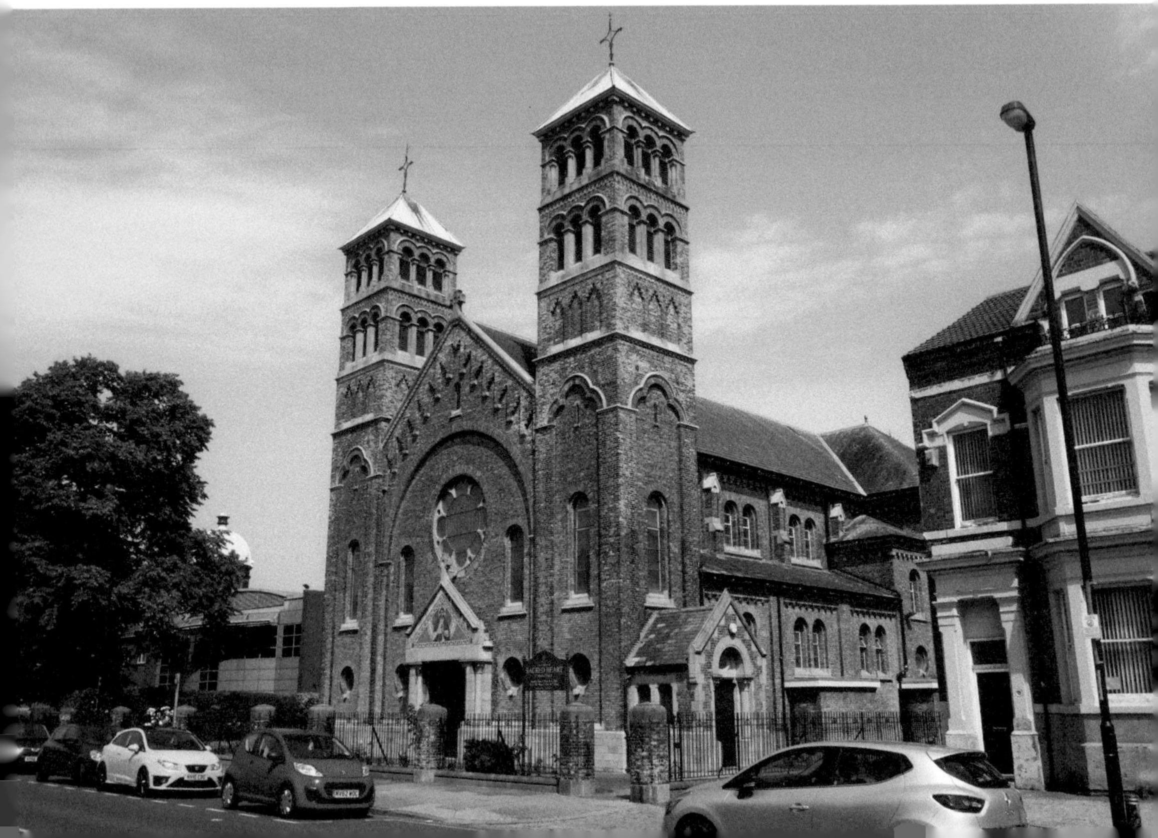

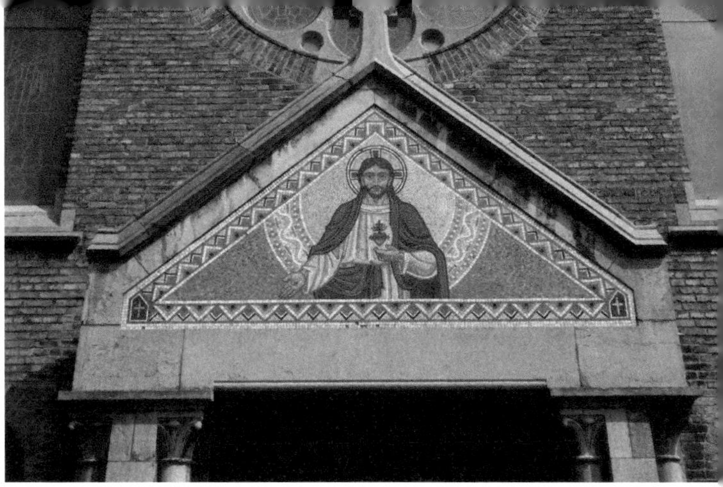

The mosaic pediment of the Sacred Heart Church.

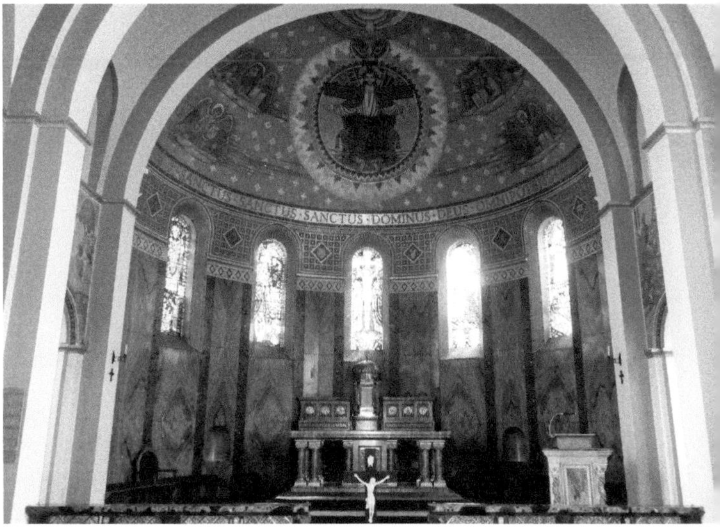

The high altar and gleaming chancel mosaics.

composed of Romanesque arcades. Between them, the west face is articulated with ornamental brickwork and a sweeping blind arch that encloses a colossal rose window and entrance. A triangular pediment is supported by stone shafts with waterleaf capitals. The tympanum of the pediment is filled with a glorious mosaic depicting Christ.

The interior is a modern interpretation of a Romanesque basilica, culminating in a semicircular chancel with a domed ceiling. Emulating the abbey church in Belgium, the walls of the chancel are lined with green marble, emphasising the spectacular marble and gold altar (1954). The chancel dome is covered with a glittering mosaic depicting Christ in glory. This was executed by the Manchester firm of Ludwig Oppenheimer Ltd in 1961–67, along with equally dazzling mosaics throughout the interior. Those in the transepts represent the Resurrection and Transfiguration of Christ, while the spandrels of the arcades depict local saints and clerics. Together, these images form a unified artistic scheme, executed in an archaic style that evokes the early days of Christian worship. The radiant stained-glass windows were made at Harry Clarke's studio in Dublin (*c.* 1960) with bright, jewel-like colours.

St Joseph's Church, Marton Road (1933–34)

St Joseph's Church was built to serve an expanding suburb of Middlesbrough. Like many Catholic churches of its era, it was designed in the Romanesque style, consciously evoking the early Christian architecture of Italy and the eastern Mediterranean. The decision to use an early medieval, Continental style was no doubt inspired by the spectacular Church of the Sacred Heart, which had recently been completed on Linthorpe Road.

Middlesbrough was expanding southwards in the 1920s and demand arose for a Catholic church in the Acklam area. A temporary tin church was built in 1925, followed by a school in 1927, designed by Thomas Rodgers of Darlington. The present church was built at an estimated cost of £7,000 to designs by Thomas A. Crawford of London. The builder was Frank Spink of Bridlington.

Breaking with liturgical tradition, St Joseph's Church was oriented with its chancel at the west end in order to give the building an entrance on Marton Road. Built of brown brick with red-brick dressings, the body consists of an aisled nave, robust towers and a semicircular apse. The south-east tower is an Italian-style campanile or bell tower with an open belfry at its summit. The doorway to the campanile features a mosaic tympanum bearing the arms of Pius XI, who was Pope when the church was built. Linking the towers is a columned portico characteristic of early Italian churches such as Santi Vincenzo e Anastasio alle Tre Fontane in Rome (1130–43).

Inside, the nave is divided by round, tapering piers in Byzantine style. The arches are built of exposed brick, similar to those at St Francis' Church at Acklam. The sanctuary and Lady Chapel are lined with glittering mosaics, echoing the interiors of Byzantine churches. The tall reredos, with a mosaic depiction of the Last Supper, is enshrined within a marble ciborium, a canopy supported by columns.

Receiving further commissions from the Catholic Church, Crawford produced very similar designs for St Francis of Assisi at Acklam (1935) and the Holy Name

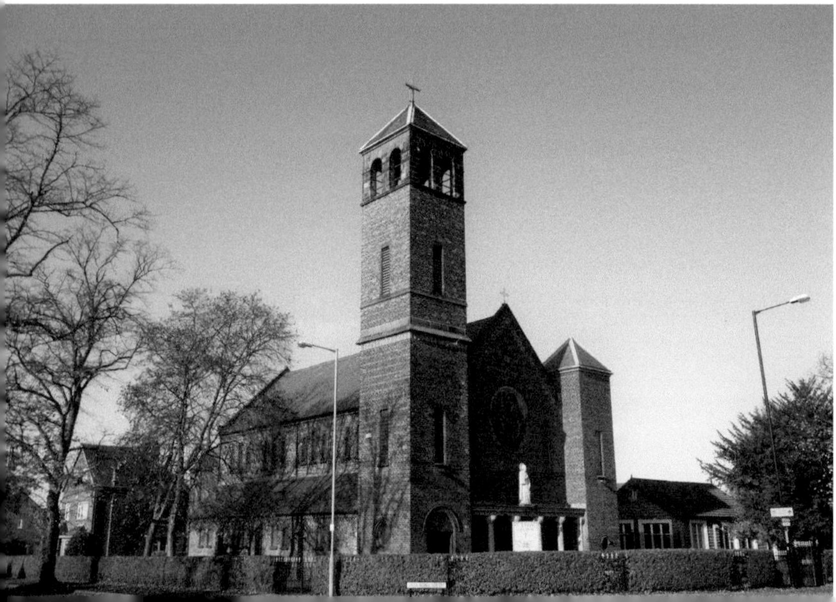

St Joseph's Church (1933–34), in neo-Romanesque style.

of Mary at Linthorpe (1938). Each of his Middlesbrough churches was archaic in conception, recalling early Christian architecture and featuring an Italianate campanile. In each case, however, these elements were reworked to reflect a modern sensibility.

Kitching Building, Albert Road (1936)

The architecture of Albert Road is richly varied, but no building is more distinctive than the stark edifice at Nos 23–25. Designed by local architects Kitching and Archibald as offices for their architectural practice, the building was daringly modern for its time. Stylistically, the design is difficult to define, displaying characteristics of two emergent styles of the interwar period.

One interpretation would see it as an early example of modernist influence in the North East. Emerging in Europe, modernism was a radical movement in architecture that rejected historical styles and pursued an aesthetic of extreme minimalism. The façade is emphatically planar, broken only by a central recession, which forms an indented entrance. Horizontal strip windows run across the façade, following the angles of the central portal. The windows have no visible supports, indicating that the façade is supported by the building's structural frame. This fulfils Le Corbusier's principle of the 'free façade', which he employed to brilliant effect in his Villa Savoye near Paris (1928–31). Further details, such as the square pediment above the entrance, suggest the influence of another modernist building, the Shilling House in Newcastle (1925).

However, the façade is relieved by two streaking mullions in the central bay and the suggestion of a ziggurat at the roofline. Taking all these elements into account, the building can be interpreted as a very severe example of art deco design, a style that was showcased at the *Exposition des arts decoratifs* in Paris (1925) and which became synonymous with the Jazz Age. Indeed, Kitching would later design a more emphatic art deco building for the Ralph Sparks Daylight Bakery at Stockton in 1938.

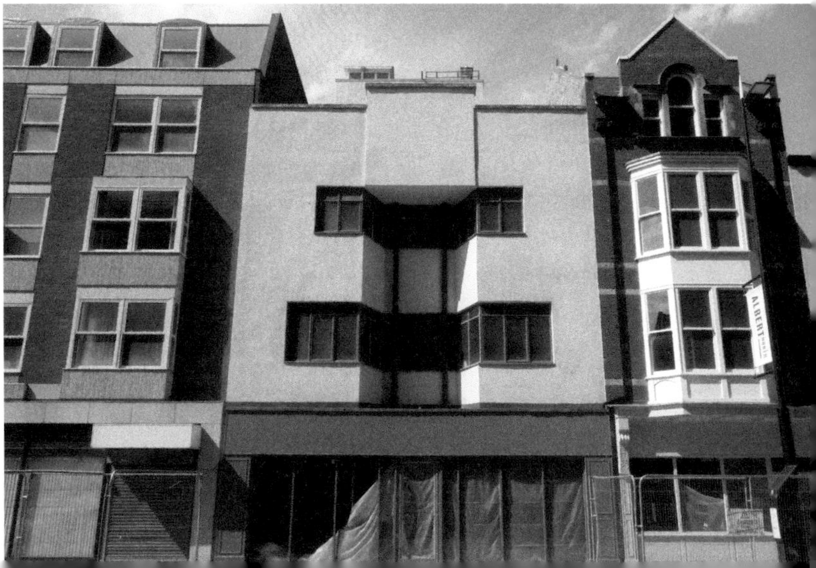

The austere façade of the Kitching Building (1936).

The Admiralty took over the building in 1939, using it as the Royal Navy's headquarters on the Tees during the Second World War. Considered an eyesore by some, the building has survived a period of neglect and threats of demolition. A recent restoration has improved its external appearance and it is hoped that the building will be valued for its advanced design and its connection with Kitching, a prolific architect, town councillor and mayor of Middlesbrough in 1943–44. His architectural practice still survives as the Dewjoc Partnership.

York House, Borough Road (1937–38)

York House was designed as a splendid new headquarters for the Joseph Constantine Shipping Co. and stands directly opposite the former Technical College that was funded by Joseph Constantine. Like the college, York House was designed by Graham R. Dawbarn of London, here working with Kitching & Co. of Middlesbrough. It was built on a steel frame, making use of shipyard technologies, and clad in a combination of brick and artificial stone. Although the construction method was modern, the aesthetic was historicist, reprising the Jacobethan style, which derived its repertory from the Elizabethan and Jacobean styles of the English Renaissance (1550–1625). By the 1930s, architects were increasingly using modern vocabularies, due in part to the influence of European modernism, but the Jacobethan style was still used sporadically.

The broad frontage is dominated by full-height bay windows, powerfully framing the entrance. The door is deeply recessed within heavy mouldings in artificial stone. The Constantine arms are displayed above the doorway, emphasising that the company was, and remains, a family-owned business. The company's emblem, a flag with a 'C' motif, is represented in each window. Spanning the façade is an extraordinary band of quatrefoils and lozenges, a feature that was possibly inspired by the approach walls at All Saints' Church, which display similar details.

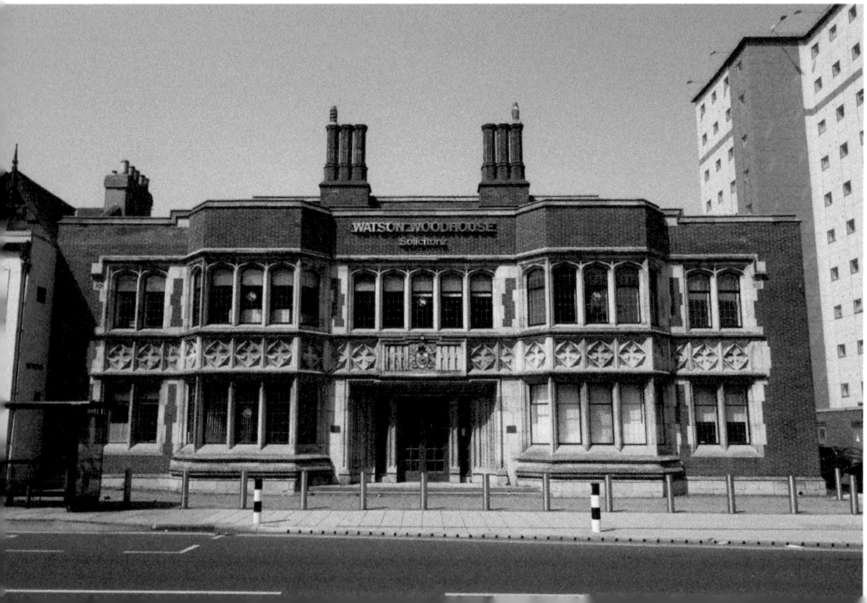

York House (1937–38), a late expression of Jacobethan style.

Octagonal chimney stacks complete the design. Despite its historicist details, the building reflects the grid-like formality of its underlying structural frame. The design of York House was curiously anachronistic, not least because the building stands opposite the quasi-modernist edifice of the Constantine Building. The interior features panelled offices and a fine oak staircase with spiral-twist balusters.

Holy Name of Mary, The Avenue (1937–38)

The Holy Name of Mary is one of several churches in the diocese of Middlesbrough designed by Thomas A. Crawford of London. Echoing his church of St Joseph, the design is a modern interpretation of the Romanesque style. As such, it evokes the forms of early Christian architecture, but also meets the twentieth-century demand for simple, functional buildings.

Marist fathers established a temporary tin church and school on this site in 1905. The present church was built in 1937–38 and the tin church was retained as a parish room until the present hall was built in 1974. The church consists of an aisled nave, south-west tower and a long sanctuary. Although the form is severe, the brickwork adds visual interest, consisting of thin red bricks laid with five courses of stretchers and one of headers. Plain parapets conceal the pitched roofs, giving the impression that the church is composed of cubic masses, in the manner of modernist buildings.

Romanesque arcades divide the interior, but the aisles are reduced to narrow passages to create a wider nave. The resulting impression of great internal space is enhanced by the absence of any partition between nave and sanctuary. South of the sanctuary is a small Lady Chapel with a hemispherical ceiling. The glazing consists of dimpled panes with art deco designs in blue glass. A notable feature of the interior is a series of oil paintings by Sir Frank Brangwyn (1867–1956), representing the Stations of the Cross. These were commissioned by Father John William Jones in 1938. Brangwyn reportedly did the paintings as a gift, charging only for transport. In 1945, he painted *The Last Supper*, which is mounted on the east wall.

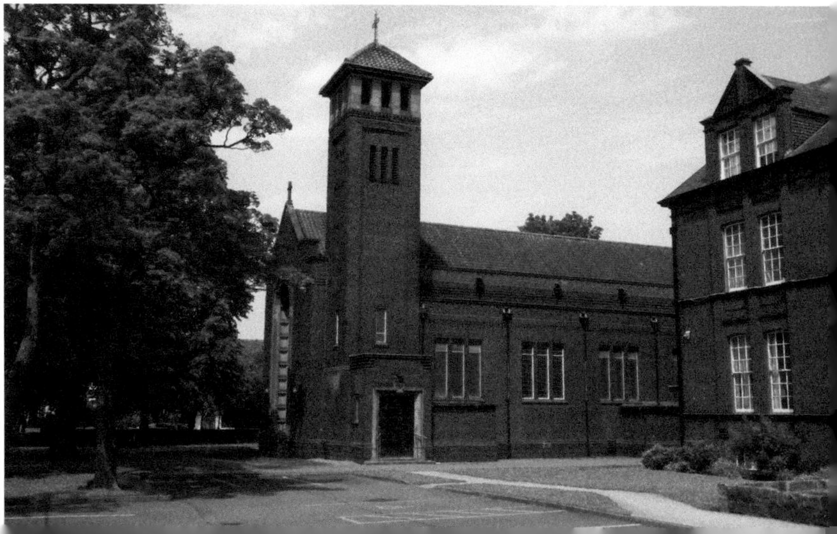

Holy Name of Mary (1937–38), continuing the Romanesque tradition.

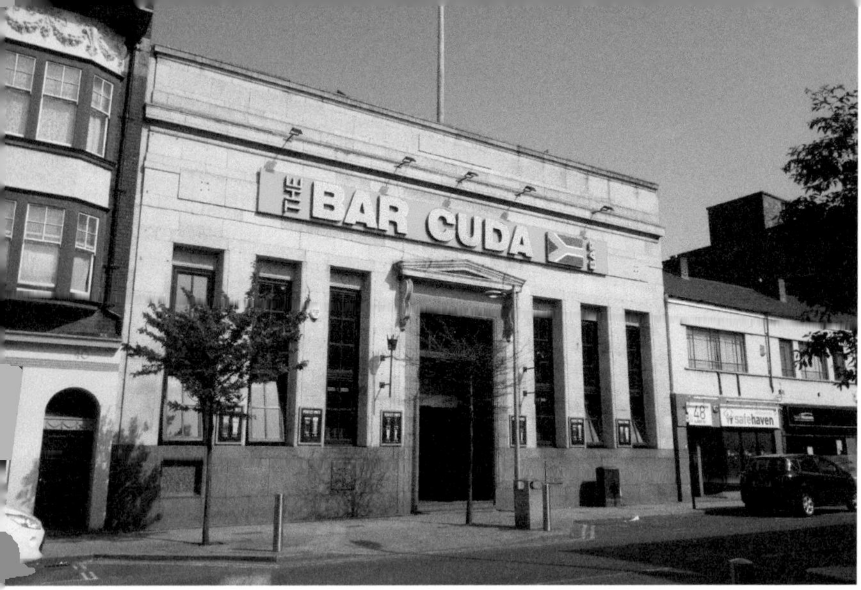

The former National Provincial Bank (1938).

National Provincial Bank, Albert Road (1938)

The National Provincial Bank sold its grand building on Cleveland Street in 1936 and erected a new branch in the more central location of Albert Road. This smaller building takes the form of a pavilion in the stripped classical style, a modernised form of classicism. Raised on a plinth of grey granite, the building comprises one storey, emphasised by tall windows cut into a façade of Portland stone. The minimal ornamentation includes a shallow pediment over the door and blocks of rock-faced granite embedded in the plinth.

The magnificent bronze doors display motifs taken from Ancient Greek coins, complementing the building's classical attributes. The doors were designed by W. F. C. Holden (*fl. ca.* 1914–42), who became architect to the National Provincial Bank in the mid-1930s and designed similar doors for many other branches. After a corporate merger, the building became a branch of the National Westminster Bank. Now operating as a bar, the former banking hall has been much altered, but the exterior contributes to the characterful architecture of Albert Road.

St Martin of Tours Church, Acklam Road (1940)

This wartime church is further evidence of the extraordinary variety to be found in Middlesbrough's ecclesiastical architecture. St Martin's Church was designed by George Edward Charlewood (1890–1962) of Newcastle, the son of Victorian architect Henry Clement Charlewood (1857–1943). Whilst his father was a master of the Gothic Revival, Charlewood produced a modern design that reflected the latest developments in European architecture, as well as the austerity of the war years.

By this date, traditional styles of architecture seemed antiquated even for churches, forcing architects to develop new modes of expression. Built of brick in

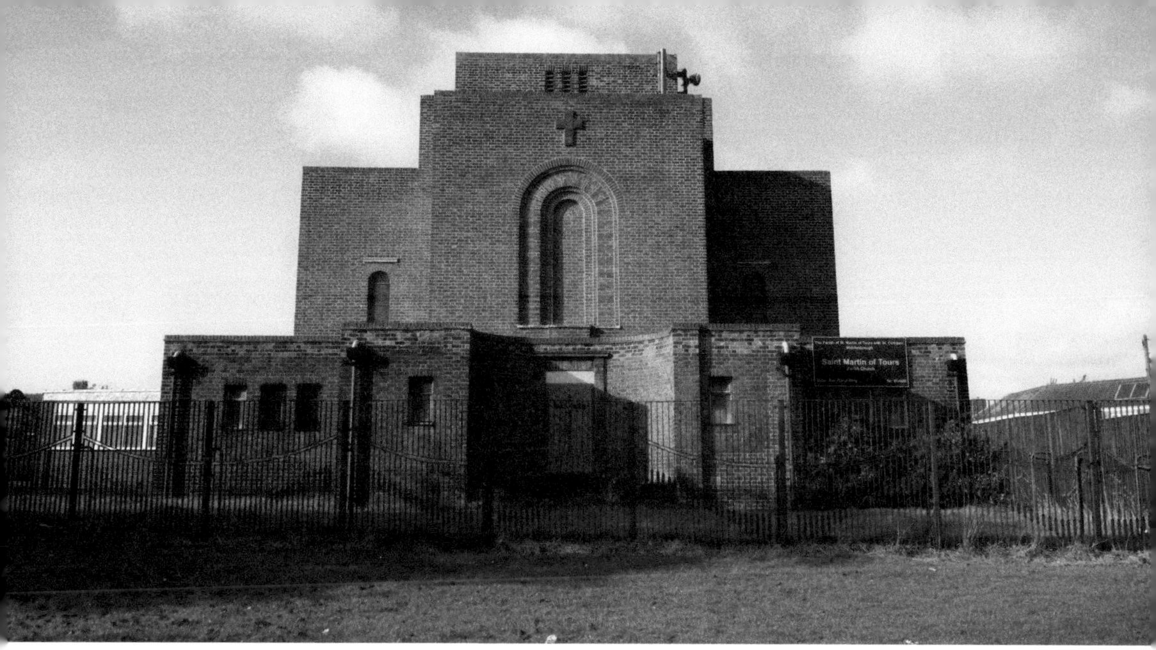

St Martin of Tours Church (1940), a place of worship for the modern age.

powerful cubic forms, St Martin's Church shows the influence of Dutch Modern architecture of the 1930s, specifically the work of the Amsterdam School. The plan is fairly conventional, with a nave, aisles and transepts, but these elements have been rendered as abstract masses in plain brick.

An eastern entrance, now blocked, is set within a concave recession, perhaps showing the influence of Upmeads in Stafford (1908), an innovative domestic design by Edgar Wood. The masses at the east end build up to a stolid tower, flanked by immense transepts. Each of these components is flat-roofed. The west face, an expanse of stark brick, is relieved by a blind Romanesque arch and a brick cross. While some would find the result overly utilitarian, it produced a bold and uncompromising church for the modern age. The interior is a minimalist rendition of traditional prototypes, with exposed-brick piers and a spartan chancel arch.

Little Theatre, The Avenue (1957)

Middlesbrough's Little Theatre was the first new playhouse built in England after the Second World War. Efforts to build a permanent theatre were frustrated by the National Austerity Programme, which prohibited building except for essential purposes. These restrictions were lifted in 1954 and a building fund for a permanent venue was launched the following year. The final cost was £54,357.

Designed by London architects Elder & De Pierro, the theatre is a modernist pavilion with a strict rectangular plan and minimal detailing. The aesthetic is softened by the use of warm brick, exemplifying the more humane form of modernism developed by post-war British architects. Dominated by a horizontal strip of glazing, the façade is an asymmetrical assembly of projecting

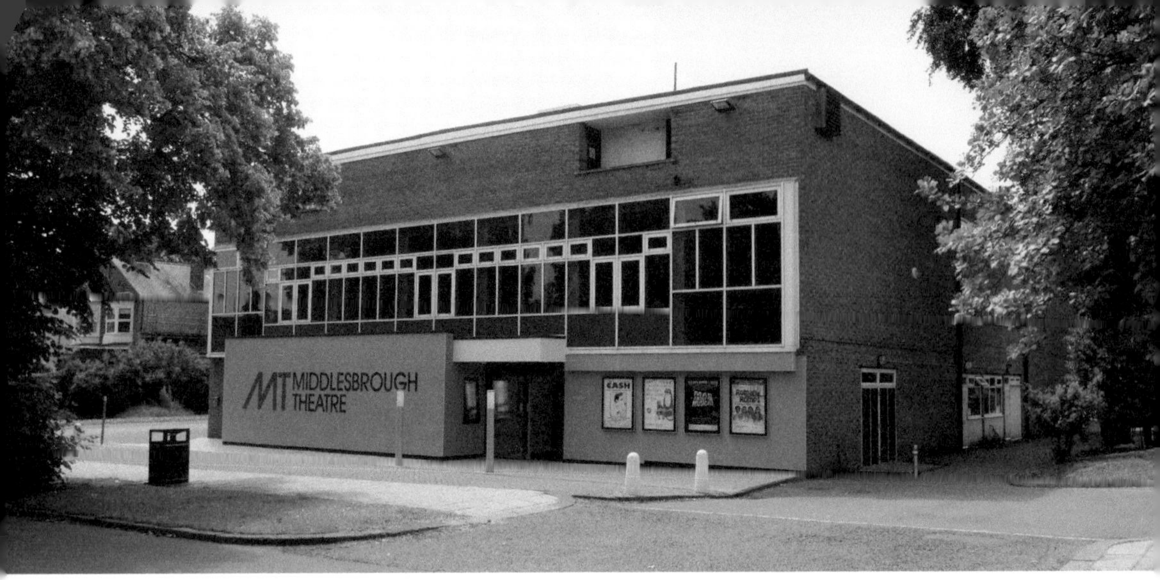

Middlesbrough's Little Theatre (1957).

and receding planes. The auditorium had seating for 484 patrons and a stage measuring 70 feet by 40 feet. By the mid-1960s, the cost of running the theatre had become too high and it was taken over by Teesside Corporation. The building was renamed the Middlesbrough Theatre in 1996 and it continues with this name today.

Police Headquarters, Dunning Road (1961–62)

Exemplifying Middlesbrough's post-war architecture, the police headquarters on Dunning Road were opened in 1962 to unify the various departments of the local police force. Standing vigilant over Victoria Square, the building embodied the principles of modernism, a twentieth-century movement that advocated formulaic rationalism and the use of industrial materials.

Middlesbrough's police force had previously occupied rooms in the Town Hall, but successive chiefs had expressed horror at the accommodation. As part of a five-year plan required by the Home Office (1949), the Watch and Licensing Committee developed plans for a new headquarters. Grange Road Methodist Church was demolished to make way for the building and plans were prepared by Borough Engineer and Surveyor J. A. Kenyon, assisted by the Chief Constable, in February 1960. This prismatic edifice was built by A. Monk & Co. for £237,313.

The building was split into two distinct masses, a six-storey administration block and a two-storey amenity block with an undulating profile. The first housed the various police divisions, as well as cells, a firing range and a gymnasium, while the second provided lecture rooms, games rooms, canteen and garage. The main block was a large cubic edifice, built on a reinforced concrete frame with glass curtain walls. The ground floor was cut away to expose the structural columns and the façades were composed as geometric grids. This vocabulary was derived from Ludwig Mies van der Rohe (1886–1969), the internationally renowned architect of New York's Seagram Building (1958). Introducing a mannerist element,

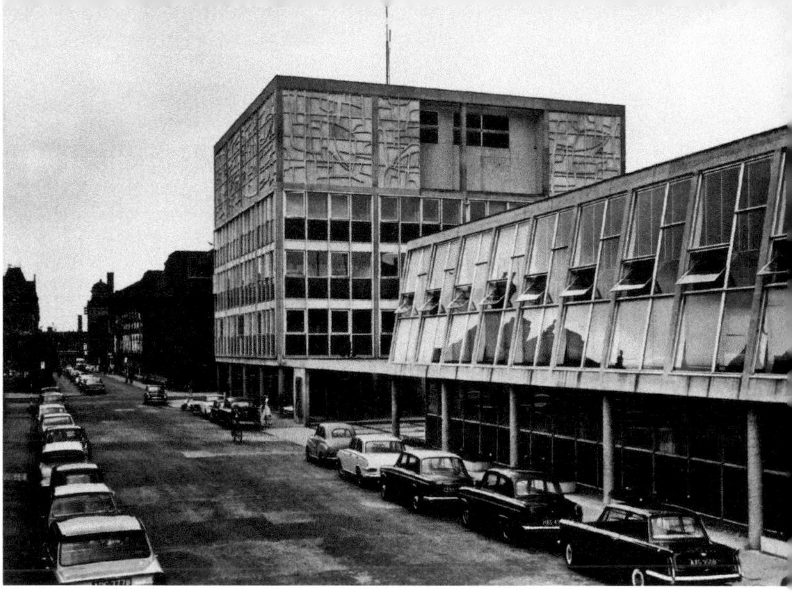

Police Headquarters (1961–62). (Middlesbrough Libraries and Information)

however, the building featured high screen-walling, ornamented with abstract reliefs in cast concrete. Overall, the building's modernist design complemented that of the neighbouring magistrates' court, although the resulting effect of faceless uniformity was rather Orwellian. Despite being one of Middlesbrough's better modern buildings, the entire complex was demolished in 2013.

St Mary's Cathedral, Dalby Way, Coulby Newham (1982–87)

Middlesbrough's Catholic community worshipped at St Mary's Cathedral on Sussex Street for over a century. However, population exodus after the Second World War saw many of the faithful relocate to new suburban housing estates. In 1976, Bishop McClean conceived the idea of building a new cathedral at Coulby Newham, an expanding suburb south of the town. The initial plans were drawn by Frank B. Swainston, whose practice was responsible for several local churches. However, Swainston died in 1982 and his partner, Peter Fenton, formalised the design and furnishings.

The complex consists of an interconnected cathedral, church hall and presbytery. Accommodating 700 people, the cathedral is built on a steel frame, but clad in light-brown brick, which helps to integrate the building into its suburban setting. The church lies under an irregular roof, which is fractured into separate planes. Resembling a fragmented pyramid, the building is illuminated by strips of glazing that slice through the roof. With its fragmentary form, the church reveals the possible influence of deconstructivist architecture of the 1980s, which sought to challenge the paradigms of architecture by exploding the myth of pure form. Two vertical structures, abstract obelisks, frame the entrance. The taller of these functions as a campanile, with three bells suspended from it.

The interior was arranged according to the liturgical principles laid down by the Second Vatican Council (1962–65) and is a broad fan-shape with a raked floor. The plan was conceived by McClean's successor, Bishop Augustine Harris,

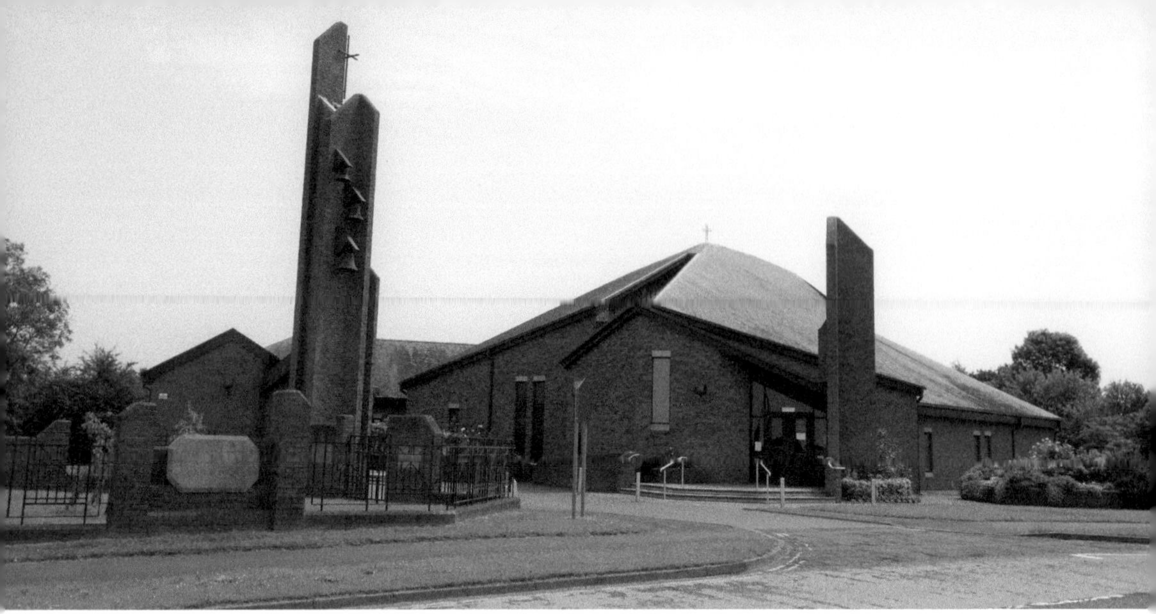

St Mary's Cathedral (1982–87), sheltered beneath its fragmentary roofscape.

based on his experience of the advantages and disadvantages of the cathedral-in-the-round at Liverpool. The walls are of bare brick and the ceiling is a series of interlocking geometric plates. Behind the altar is a reredos painted by Bob Brumby, a complex work in which Christian iconography dissolves into a spectrum of colour symbolising the Resurrection. According to the artist, an abstract design was chosen in order to foreground the altar and make it 'sing out'.

Middlesbrough Institute of Modern Art (2002–07)

The Middlesbrough Institute of Modern Art is a gallery of modern and contemporary art designed as part of an urban regeneration scheme to revitalise the heart of Middlesbrough. Opened in January 2007, the gallery is generally known as 'mima', in reference to New York's Museum of Modern Art or 'MOMA'. A symbol of Teesside's post-industrial renaissance, the £20m project reflected mayor Ray Mallon's ambition to transform Middlesbrough into a 'designer label town'.

Responding to the collapse of traditional industries, many towns and cities have emulated Bilbao's Guggenheim Museum (1997) by pursuing a strategy of culture-led regeneration to stimulate economic and social growth. In 2002, Middlesbrough held an international competition to create a master plan for a new civic space and institute of modern art. The competition was won by Dutch architectural practice Erick van Egeraat Associated Architects, which has produced striking buildings around the globe. Linking these projects is an expressive, almost baroque treatment of modernist forms. Volumetric collisions, intersecting planes and a degree of ornamentation define an approach the architect has described as 'Modern Baroque'.

In essence, mima is a democratic interpretation of the 'white cube' art gallery, an archetype which some have criticised as elitist. It consists of two interpenetrating volumes, each clad in white Turkish limestone, but the principal façade is reduced to a glass screen, creating a more accessible building. The transparent façade reveals a public atrium containing a shop and café. A rusticated limestone wall, daringly suspended, plunges into the building. This acts as an ordering device, separating the public area from the five gallery spaces, workshop and offices beyond. The limestone wall shifts intriguingly in texture, while a diagonal slash across its surface provides a graphic indicator of the position of the staircase.

The café features tableware and cutlery by Japanese ceramicist Takeshi Yasuda, while the furniture was designed by Gijs Bakker, co-founder of Holland's fashionable Droog design collective. The shop, designed by Michael Rowe, features a black Corian shelving installation by artist Andrew Miller and Colin Williams Design. A sculptural play of angles, it was inspired by the geometry of the building itself. The presence of spaces of leisure and consumption indicate that, in twenty-first-century consumer culture, museums and galleries are increasingly forced to compete with entertainment and retail environments.

Van Egeraat received a RIBA Award for his design, which the jury described as 'a very elegant and enjoyable building which reconciles the urban aspirations of Middlesbrough with the need for a quality, carefully crafted gallery'. The enlarged public square was designed in conjunction with Dutch landscape architects West 8. Van Egeraat's projects typically respond to their historical context. In this case, oxidised metal plates set into the grass evoke Middlesbrough's history as a dynamic capital of iron and steel production. The master plan has succeeded in reconfiguring the town centre, creating one of the largest civic spaces in Europe. In this revitalised setting, the Victorian Town Hall that exemplifies Middlesbrough's triumphant past stands in dynamic relationship with the resplendent gallery that anticipates its future.

Middlesbrough Institute of Modern Art (2002–07), integrated into a newly formed public space.

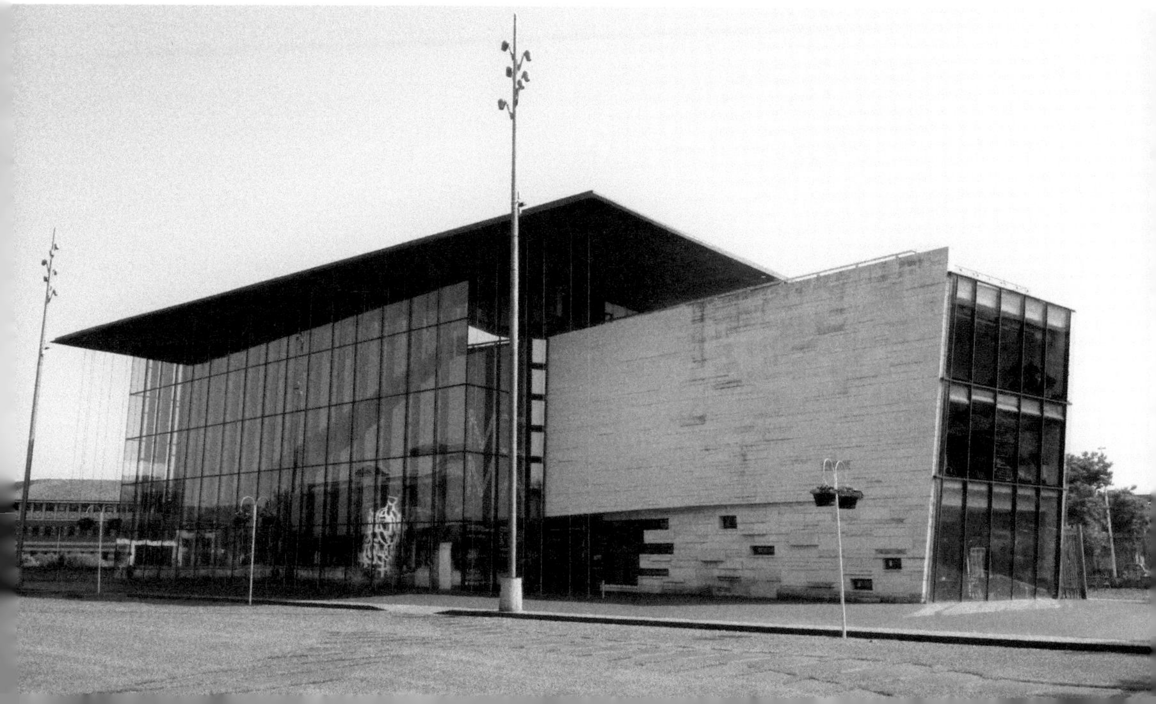

Bibliography

Black, I. S., 'National Provincial Bank Buildings in North-East England in the later Nineteenth Century.' *Durham Archaeological Journal*, vol. 17, 2003, pp. 63-82.

Brandwood, Geoffrey, *Temple Moore: an architect of the late Gothic Revival* (Stamford: Paul Watkins, 1997).

Briggs, Asa, *Victorian Cities* (London: Odhams Press, 1964).

Buckley, Cheryl, 'Modernity, tradition and the design of the "industrial village" of Dormanstown 1917–1921.' *Journal of Design History*, vol. 23, no. 1, 2010, pp. 21-41.

Carson, Robert, *A Short History of Middlesbrough* (Middlesbrough: Middlesbrough Borough Council, 1977).

Cunningham, Colin, *Alfred Waterhouse, 1830-1905: biography of a practice* (Oxford: Clarendon Press, 1992).

Curry, Rosemary and Kirk, Sheila, *Philip Webb in the North: the architecture of Philip Webb and furnishings by William Morris, 1863-1900* (Middlesbrough: Teesside Polytechnic Press, 1984).

Fawcett, Bill, *History of North Eastern Railway Architecture* (North Eastern Railway Association, 2005).

Faulkner, Thomas, Berry, Helen and Gregory, Jeremy, *Northern Landscapes: representations and realities of North-East England* (Woodbridge: Boydell, 2010).

Felstead, Alison, *et al., RIBA Directory of British Architects 1834-1900* (London: Mansell, 1993).

Harper, Roger H., *Victorian Architectural Competitions: An Index to British and Irish Architectural Competitions in* The Builder *1843-1900* (London: Mansell, 1983).

Harrison, B.J.D. and Pattenden, D.W., *Middlesbrough's History in Maps: an album of maps and plans from the 17th to the 20th centuries* (Middlesbrough: Cleveland & Teeside Local History Society, 1980).

Hood, Harold, *Middlesbrough Pictorial & Industrial: representing some of the pictorial aspects of a great industrial district* (Middlesbrough: Hood & Co., 1926).

Hudson, Martyn and Fraser Gupta, Anthea, *'A Palace for Paupers': the Holgate Workhouse 1875-1930* (Middlesbrough: Black Light Engine Room Press, 2018).

Judge, Edward, *Dorman Long: a concise history* (Middlesbrough: Dorman Long, 1992).

Lillie, William, *History of Middlesbrough: An Illustration of the Evolution of English Industry* (Middlesbrough: Middlesbrough Corporation, 1968).

Lock, Max (ed.), *The County Borough of Middlesbrough: Survey and Plan* (Middlesbrough: Middlesbrough Corporation, 1946).

Moorsom, Norman, *The Anglican Church in Teesside: an introductory historical survey and directory* (Middlesbrough: Norman Moorsom, 1970).

Pearson, Lynne F., 'The Architecture of Entertainment Run Riot: William Hope of Newcastle, 1862-1907.' *Northern History*, 27, 1991, pp. 184-97.

Pevsner, Nikolaus, *Yorkshire, The North Riding* (New Haven: Yale University Press, 2002).

Pollard, Anthony J. (ed.), *Middlesbrough: town and community 1830-1950* (Stroud: Sutton, 1996).

Street, George Edmund, *Brick and Marble in the Middle Ages: notes of a tour in the north of Italy* (London: John Murray, 1855).

Stubbs, Ian and Parker, Jenny, *Middlesbrough: A Century of Change* (Stroud: Tempus Publishing, 2006).

Stubley, Peter, *The Churches and the Iron and Steel Industry in Middlesbrough 1890-1914* (Durham: Durham University Theses, 1979).

Van Loo, Anne, *Dictionnaire de l'architecture en Belgique: de 1830 à nos jours* (Bruxelles: Fonds Mercator, Bruxelles, 2003).

Index